SAVORING
THE
WISDOM OF
PROVERBS

SAVORING THE WISDOM OF PROVERBS

LOUIS GOLDBERG

MOODY PRESS
CHICAGO

ISBN: 0-8024-7636-8

1 2 3 4 5 6 Printing/BC/Year 94 93 92 91 90

Printed in the United States of America

CONTENTS

ACKNOWLEDGMENTS

I am indebted to my Jewish background and training, which put great emphasis upon the necessity of repentance from wrong deeds, involvement with prayer on a daily basis, and, most important, the performance of the *misvot*, which, translated literally, is the practice of a devout life-style. However, the *misvot* is not merely a "tit for tat" with the Almighty wherein a person might say, "I did my good deed for the day, so please bless me accordingly." Rather, everyone is encouraged by the religious leaders to live piously in the here and now out of love for fellow men and God.

In the traditional Jewish sense, the rabbinical leaders viewed the wisdom of Proverbs as the means by which a person is enabled to live a moral life. Only in this way can one have the greatest joy and happiness. As a child and young person, I was already exposed to some of the morals expressed in the book of Proverbs.

In later years, as a teacher, I have shared the truths of the book of Proverbs to countless students. In the give and take of the classroom, many of the lessons from this book have not been easy to digest, and in the ensuing discussions both teacher and students have learned much as we have permitted this portion of the Word to speak to our hearts. I am eternally grateful for what has been accomplished in our lives in the classroom, as well as out on the highways of life. As this commentary goes forth to you, the reader, my hope is that you too will benefit greatly through what has gone into this work.

I am extremely thankful to Brenda Combs, who typed the original draft, corrected the numerous editions, and has finally produced the final manuscript. Above all, I am grateful for the patience of a loving wife throughout the many hours of manuscript preparation. Her encouragement and "her works" have brought her praise (Proverbs 31:31a).

PREFACE

Some 2,500 years ago Daniel prophesied that in the last days "many will go here and there to increase knowledge" (Daniel 12:4). We live in a day when knowledge is exploding at such a rate that no one could master it all in a lifetime. But even though man has gone to the moon, sent probes to distant planets, and discovered the smallest life forms in the microscopic world, is he any better morally or spiritually?

Three millennia ago Solomon penned what is the motto for most of the book of Proverbs: "The fear of the Lord is the beginning of knowledge" (1:7). Solomon does not advocate being in terror of the Lord; rather, he insists that we begin with God by accepting, knowing, and loving Him. The knowledge He provides enables us to live in obedience to His will.

By no means is the believer to despise the wisdom of this world, for all truth discovered through legitimate research is God's truth. Because He created the universe, we can only scratch the surface of the knowledge that has been present since the creation. However, the knowledge man gains from the use of his reason and through scientific method must be considered in the light of what has been created and provided. When we use this knowledge for man's benefit today, we have to realize who is the source of all knowledge: the Lord.

Many of God's people have some apprehension when they get into the book of Proverbs or the other books of wisdom: Ecclesiastes and Job. While Proverbs deals with the practicalities of life, the other two books are more speculative, handling the problems of evil, the prosperity of the wicked, why the righteous suffer, and rewards and punishment. The feeling persists that these are not the books to turn to for spiritual food.

The book of Psalms is easily read, and its writers speak to readers' hearts. The book of Joshua makes for easy reading, with narrative that is considered interesting. Wisdom Literature, however, seems to leave believers baffled because sometimes this material requires a great deal of effort to understand. Even if the reader has a grasp of what the writers of Proverbs seek to impart, the question still remains as to how to read the wisdom of Proverbs profitably and have the blessings God wants to provide.

The Introduction to this book provides instruction in understanding the way wisdom is presented in Proverbs: getting a handle on similes; appreciating the parallelism of Hebrew poetry; recognizing wisdom in its many kinds of "dresses"; and how to apply this knowledge in interpreting the wisdom of Proverbs. With a grasp of these principles, the reader is guided into the first nine chapters. Wisdom spends a lot of time and effort instructing the naive, the child, and the teenager to help each young person be victorious over the problems they are facing and will face as mature adults.

The teachings of Proverbs 1-9 are considered: to understand the *goal* of wisdom in her outreach; why the fruits of wisdom are so important; how the disciple can be wise in the ways of the Lord, as well as in the practicalities of life; the burden the father carries in his spiritual leadership of the family; the call for chastity, with good instruction in how to avoid the temptation of immorality; the abundant folly we run into and how we can avoid it; and why and how we should respond to the call of wisdom to avoid "folly's cursed crumbs."

The concluding chapters (8-12) consider the teachings of Proverbs 10-31 topically: the dynamics of the relationship between God and man; the pleasurable and undesirable emotions common to humanity; what Wisdom has to say about relationships within the family; wise and foolish speech, laziness, and folly; and, finally, what wisdom says about the issues of life and death.

To make Proverbs easier to understand, the *New International Version* is used throughout the book. Frequently, however, I provide a literal translation from the Hebrew so as to accurately render what the original language declares, and occasionally I introduce another Bible translation.

Wisdom seeks to have her way, by taunt or tease, encouragement or direct command, so as to direct the reader's life. To the unbeliever, guidance is given to enable a response to Wisdom's pleas to come to faith. The believer, however, has in the wisdom of Proverbs the guidelines for godly living in this life and for demonstrating a righteousness that will affect both rich and poor, national leaders and lay people, and even impact the direction a nation will take.

The Psalms can take us into the audience chamber of the Most High, and His communion with us can make our hearts glow. The wisdom of Proverbs, however, "makes the face shine" as we penetrate into the many levels and ranks of our society. Both are necessary truths, but the latter is what makes our faith practical. So, dear reader, welcome to the world of the wisdom of Proverbs. My fervent wish is that this fascinating book will become a part of you and that, guided by the wisdom of God, your testimony can be strengthened as you impact your world of friends for the Lord.

The fear of the Lord is the beginning of knowledge,
but fools despise wisdom and discipline.

INTRODUCTION

According to the biblical records, three thousand proverbs are ascribed to King Solomon (1 Kings 4:32). Although some may question whether this king actually wrote these proverbs, good evidence exists that he did and that they comprise the bulk of the books of Proverbs and Ecclesiastes. Our Savior's word concerning "Solomon's wisdom" is a testimony to his great reputation (Matthew 12:42). However, only Jesus could refer to Himself as "one greater than Solomon" (Luke 11:31).

Solomon was one of Israel's most illustrious kings. Upon inheriting the kingdom from his father, David, he increased its boundaries and exercised a practical wisdom among his many subjects. He was noted for his literary pursuits, musical talents, and scientific curiosity. Besides the proverbs, 1,005 songs also came from his pen. "He described plant life, from the cedar of Lebanon to the hyssop that grows out of walls"; "he also taught about animals and birds, reptiles and fish." Men and women of fame and fortune came to hear his wisdom and seek his counsel (1 Kings 10:1-25).

The basis of Solomon's stature is rooted in an incident at the very beginning of his reign. After presiding at the great sacrificial offering at Gibeon soon after he as-

13

sumed the throne, this king had a dream that was to be
the turning point in his life (1 Kings 3:1-15). In his dream,
the question by God was: "Ask for whatever you want me
to give you." The Lord made no reservation or condition;
it was a blank check. Solomon humbled himself and
asked for a discerning heart that would enable him to
have wisdom, knowledge, and the ability "to distinguish
between right and wrong" (1 Kings 3:9). Because he did
not ask for long life, riches, or vengeance upon his enemies, as most young kings of that time would have done,
God not only gave him the gift of wisdom but riches and
honor as well.

This request for wisdom eventually gave mankind
more than the mere wisdom of Solomon. His writings and
proverbs that appear in the Bible are a part of the inspired
record and constitute God's Word for us today. The application of wisdom in Solomon's experiences during his
lifetime has crystalized to give us the best possible view
of life; we can have divine assurance for sound decisions
for life in accordance with His will.

In a sense, we are all confronted by God, as was Solomon, to make right decisions. He comes to each of us
with the same question He once asked Solomon: "What
do you want in life?" Some choose money. Others desire
fame, power, or lust. But how many today would request
divine wisdom, as did Solomon? And yet this is the decision that leads to salvation, the knowledge of God, the
spiritually abundant life now, and eternal life in His presence. May God grant us to seek this wisdom for ourselves.
The study of Proverbs will help us to make decisions
pleasing to God.

WISDOM IN OLD TESTAMENT REVELATION

Within the Old Testament, we note three classes of
ministers with different functions. The *priest* ministered
at the altar, offering up sacrifices on behalf of the people,
thereby representing them before God. One of his basic
tasks was to serve the people who came to worship. The
prophet had an opposite ministry. Through various ways

he received messages from God and delivered this word to the people, either through preaching or through prophecy, with its implications for the future. Therefore, the prophet represented God to the people. The functions of both priests and prophets can be seen in Jeremiah 18:18.

A third class of servants, however, is revealed in the same passage: the *sage* or *wise man*. His service was distinct from the prophet or priest, yet his wisdom was always in harmony with their message and function. Though the wise man did not claim inspiration for his counsel, the wisdom he possessed was given by God (Proverbs 2:6). The wise man did not predict as did the prophet, but he had a most important function within Israel by giving practical advice to those who needed it.

The person who sought wisdom did not have to speculate or act as a philosopher. Neither Old Testament wisdom nor the wisdom described in the book of James should be confused with the Greek idea of intellectual knowledge, as good as it may be at times. Biblical wisdom is not theoretical. Rather, it is a wisdom based on a revelation from the God of truth Himself. God knows every situation a person will ever experience, and His divine revelation can provide a practical knowledge that will fit all the problems of life. Therefore, the person who wishes to be wise has access to a wisdom that will help him sift right from wrong. Said the wise man of the Scriptures, "The fear of the Lord is the beginning of knowledge" (Proverbs 1:7). Since this knowledge can be applied to the problems of life, it's as if the sage adds, "See to it that you put this knowledge into practice!"

Most of Proverbs is not to be applied exclusively to the Old Testament believer. The word *Israel* occurs only once, but the term *man* (translated from *'adam*, a generic reference to all mankind) appears some forty-three times in Proverbs. With certain exceptions, therefore, the wisdom of the Old Testament is generally applicable everywhere to people of all times. The book of Proverbs is offered to all travelers along the road of life. We need not drift aimlessly in the currents of man's speculations; for those who seek it, the wisdom of God is applicable to all life's problems.

WISDOM AS A PERSON

A number of passages in Proverbs present wisdom as a person. Wisdom shouts for attention in the busy streets (1:20-23) and pleads with grace and dignity on other occasions (8:34-35). Wisdom is depicted as an agent of creation alongside God (8:22-30) and, consequently, rejoices "in his whole world" and delights "in mankind" (8:31).

This relationship between wisdom and God will be treated in a later chapter, but the emphasis here is that wisdom must not be regarded as cold counsel or as a set of instructions to be obeyed in a legalistic sense. Our attitude toward wisdom should be as one thinks and acts toward a person with sensitivities and feelings. The portrayal of wisdom as a person was intended to appeal to us as people and thereby attract our utmost interest on an interpersonal basis.

The word for wisdom in the original Hebrew is in the feminine, which is a highly suggestive concept when we consider again the presentation of wisdom as a person. Wisdom is pictured as a woman, a gracious hostess, inviting all people to her banquet (9:1-5). This kind of portrayal was designed to capture our attention, and our response to wisdom should be to respect and love her as a woman, giving her deference and honor. As such, she contrasts sharply with the adultress (7:1-27).[1]

Certainly, the women in our lives, such as our wives, mothers, and daughters, merit our love and attention, and we demonstrate our care for them by doing all those things that please them. Our attitude toward wisdom should be similar. We are to follow her guidance because we love to do so. As we hear her voice and seek her company, we find the best possible guide for this life. In making this goal the practice of our lives, we please God.

1. D. Guthrie and J. Motyer, eds., *The New Bible Commentary: Revised* (Grand Rapids: Eerdmans, 1970), p. 557.

In a keen, vivid manner, then, God has depicted for us the possibility of a relationship with wisdom. The personified wisdom speaks. Let us take heed how we listen so as to do what we hear.

THE NATURE OF A PROVERB

In the English language, many proverbs are in common use. For example, "A stitch in time, saves nine," and "If the shoe fits, wear it." The book of Proverbs also presents its sayings in distinctive form. Two prominent characteristics of this form can be summarized in the following terms: likeness and parallelism.

LIKENESS

The English title, "Proverbs," is from the Hebrew word *mashal*, meaning basically "to be like," "to resemble," or "to represent." Many of the examples of likeness use the characteristic words *like* and *as* with *so*:

> As vinegar to the teeth and smoke to the eyes,
> so is a sluggard to those who send him (10:26).

> Like snow in summer or rain in harvest,
> [so] honor is not fitting for a fool (26:1).

Other proverbs of likeness do not always use the exact words, but the form is still there:

> Like a gold ring in a pig's snout
> [so] is a beautiful woman who shows
> no discretion (11:22).

Many proverbs no doubt developed out of everyday experience, and the Lord gave the wise person a timely wisdom so that he learned well from that particular situation. The occasion for the likeness or resemblance in the proverb is dropped, but the lesson will reflect a general wisdom or draw a conclusion out of life's experiences:

Wine is a mocker and beer a brawler;
whoever is led astray by them is not wise (20:1).

Such statements are recognized general truths or conclusions, but the specific backdrop for the resemblance is gone. The reference to alcoholic drink in 20:1 is interesting when we realize that Solomon penned these words. They no doubt refer to a period in Solomon's life when he gave himself to drinking as well as to the pursuit of other so-called pleasures (Ecclesiastes 2:1-3). He learned from bitter experience, it would appear, that strong drink is deplorable.

POETIC FORM—PARALLELISM

Still another way the proverb is intended to catch our eye with striking force is its poetic presentation. Hebrew poetry did not make use of rhyme; the poetic effect is created by the use of *parallelism*. This effect can be seen in at least four ways.

Synonymous parallelism. In synonymous parallelism, the second line of poetry repeats the thought of the first line in similar words:

Pride goes before destruction,
and a haughty spirit before a fall (16:18).

The use of similar language is intended to reinforce the lesson of wisdom.

Antithetic parallelism. In antithetic parallelism, the second line of poetry is in contrast to the first:

A wise son brings joy to his father,
but a foolish son brings grief to his mother (10:1).

Diligent hands will rule,
but laziness ends in slave labor (12:24).

Presenting the proverb in this way promotes understanding of the contrast between good and evil in human behavior.

Synthetic parallelism. In synthetic parallelism, the second line of poetry continues the thought of the first line:

> He who fears the Lord has a secure fortress,
> and for his children it will be a refuge (14:26).
>
> A wicked man accepts a bribe in secret
> to pervert the course of justice (17:23).

Many times in this kind of parallelism the thought is too long for the first line and is continued in the second line.

Statement and comment. In the form of statement and comment, we note how the first line of poetry makes a statement and the second line provides an explanation of the first:

> A king's wrath is like the roar of a lion;
> he who angers him forfeits his life (20:2).

So, in one way or another, God put wisdom and practical truth into common sense by means of wit, tease, taunt, and paradox in the form of poetry to guide our lives. We do well to make these proverbs a part of our experience.

WISDOM AND ITS WARDROBE

The wisdom of Proverbs can be presented in other ways as well. Wisdom can appear in many "dresses," not just in two lines of poetry.

The *discourse* is one dress. Proverbs 1-9 is an extended discourse on wisdom in general. There is also a long warning against the temptress or "loose woman" (chapter 7), and the "good wife" is discussed in 31:10-31. A series of proverbs deals with the theme of what God considers to be the fool (26:1-12). The godly sage engages in a "numbers" proverb to explain what is hateful to God (6:16-19).

Still another dress for wisdom is what we can learn from a *historical event*, but this is rare in the book of Proverbs. One such incident appears where Solomon may refer to instruction provided by his father and mother, David and Bathsheba, after they had been humbled (4:3). Out of life's experiences they teach their son.

The *allegory* is another tool. In 5:15-18 an allegory depicts a model of chastity for the godly husband and wife through the figure of cool, fresh flowing water, so precious in an arid country. What a beautiful way to portray the never-ending love relationship of a husband for his wife. Wisdom's teaching by allegory is quite apt to convey lessons important for today.

Another form of dress is the *enigma*, or dark, obscure saying. Note the profound depth of an entire chapter of enigmas (30:1-33). In one, wisdom asks for the name of God's son (30:1-4). Viewed from the Old Testament alone, this question can indeed be a baffling one.

The wardrobe of wisdom is full and varied, making it easy to take hold of instruction and guidance in the important things of life.

How to Interpret Proverbs

Recognize the poetic techniques. Is wisdom expressed by way of likeness, allegory, or history? The simple likeness that compares the obedient ear to fine gold ornaments (25:12) is to be understood differently than the enigma of the two daughters of the leech (30:15a-b). The form helps us understand the context in which wisdom is portrayed.

Apply practical and spiritual wisdom to grasp the spiritual meaning of some proverbs. The reader should have no difficulty with the meaning of one familiar proverb:

> Trust in the Lord with all your heart
> and lean not on your own understanding;
> in all your ways acknowledge him,
> and he will make your paths straight (3:5).

However, the following likeness requires some thought, research, and a spiritual grasp:

> Like tying a stone in a sling
> is the giving of honor to a fool (26:8).

In Old Testament days a man in battle whirled a stone in his sling round and round and then released the projectile with terrific force and speed, as did David in his fight with Goliath (1 Samuel 17:49). But for a warrior to tie his stone in the sling so that it could not release would be nonsense. In the same way, it is sheer stupidity to give honor to a fool.

Consider the context. To understand the difficult picture and meaning of the leech's two daughters requires a thorough examination of 30:15c-16. Even as the leech and her offspring display a never-ending demand for blood as they attach themselves to horses and other animals, so experiences exist that demand even more than the leech. *Sheol* never seems to have enough of the dead; the barren womb yearns desperately to give birth to children; after a long drought the dry, thirsty ground demands water; and a fire out of control consumes more and more, and never seems satisfied.

Be alert to clues provided by parallelism. Parallelism is an aid in interpreting the proverb. Note two lines of the synonymous parallel that teaches generosity:

> A generous man will prosper;
> he who refreshes others will himself
>   be refreshed (11:25).

Line two of the passage indicates that, in terms of the Middle East, drought is an ever-present problem. But the farmer who knows the need for water and wisely conserves his supply when it is abundant can irrigate his fields to have a good harvest. Because he will help other farmers as well, he himself will be refreshed. In the same way, we understand the meaning of line one: there is great blessing for the one who is generous.

Note also how the clear truth of diligence comes through in an antithetic parallel:

Diligent hands will rule,
but laziness will end in slave labor (12:24).

Recognize the exception to the general rule. Although many proverbs are universal propositions, they do not cover every possible situation. Note again the lesson of diligence in 12:24. The statement by the sage is a general truth, but who is to say, even in Old Testament days, that this was true in every instance? What happened to Naboth, who only wanted to be left alone to tend his vineyard? This Israelite was killed because he had tried to mind his own business and live his own life (1 Kings 21). We live in an imperfect world where righteous believers sometimes suffer while the ungodly prosper.

AUTHORS AND DATE OF COMPOSITION

The book of Proverbs in its entirety was not written by Solomon alone, even though the title—"The Proverbs of Solomon" (1:1)—says so. But the major portion does belong to him (1 Kings 4:32). The title in 1:1 applies to the first nine chapters of the book. Proverbs 10:1 repeats the title of 1:1 and includes all material to 24:34. In 25:1 mention is made that "these are more proverbs of Solomon, copied by the men of Hezekiah king of Judah." This note indicates that more of Solomon's proverbs were added to the original book during the time of Hezekiah. Thus, Solomon appears to be the author of chapters 1-29.

Chapter 30 contains many enigmas. The reference to authorship is the statement "The sayings of Agur son of Jakeh—an oracle" (30:1). The word *Agur* could be a reference to a proper name, but neither Agur nor Jakeh occurs elsewhere in the Old Testament, and we are at a loss to further identify this person. Some have suggested that Agur is a symbolic name meaning "gatherer." If the latter is the case, it can refer to someone who gathered proverbs, possibly some additional ones belonging to Solomon. Yet the information suggests that Agur was the son of Jakeh, making it difficult to understand Agur as symbolic. We can only say that the person is not identified, but that his material is included in the Word of God.

To King Lemuel is assigned the material of chapter 31. Again, *Lemuel* could be a proper name. He could have been a king who, upon ascending the throne, was given a message by his mother in the form of a burden, or oracle. However, there is no reference to such a name in the Old Testament either. The term *lemuel* can also be symbolic, meaning "to God" or, in a sense, "Godward," depicting someone given to God. As a child, Solomon had been dedicated to God and was named Jedidiah, or "loved by the Lord" (2 Samuel 12:25). Lemuel could very well be a reference to Solomon.

If the symbolic suggestion is accepted, who then is the mother? Solomon's mother was Bathsheba, and she could have been responsible for chapter 31, including the description of the virtuous woman. Could this be possible? Yes. Though Bathsheba may not have been guiltless in the affair with David, the Bible nowhere condemns her for it, and she is not depicted as having led an immoral life.[2] She, of all people, could speak meaningfully of what a virtuous woman should be and do. It is best to say that we are not sure of the identification of King Lemuel. But if it is Solomon, we have a series of proverbs and discourses from his family.

Other materials also are a part of this book. Not only are Agur and Lemuel mentioned, but references to others are also present. For example, we note the designation "These also are sayings of the wise" (24:23), suggesting additional authors. We read of the "elders who had served . . . Solomon" (1 Kings 12:6), and the term *elder* can be a synonym for "wise man." It is possible that the men who were a part of Solomon's court could have added material of their own to the proverbs of Solomon. In fact, Agur could have been one of these very elders.

2. Charles F. Pfeiffer and Everett F. Harrison, eds., *The Wycliffe Bible Commentary* (Chicago: Moody, 1962), p. 297; Guthrie and Motyer, p. 307.

As for assigning a date to the composition and final form of the book, it is best to assume that Solomon was the author of most of the material, and that, therefore, the book of Proverbs had its beginning during the time he reigned, from 971-931 B.C. Since not all of Solomon's materials were collected during his lifetime, the proverbs that remained were gathered together and added to the book about 700 B.C., in the days of Hezekiah.

The book of Proverbs was probably in formation for more than three hundred years, from the days of Solomon to Hezekiah. The Talmud (Jewish traditions) corroborates this possibility: "Hezekiah and his colleagues wrote [that is, collected] Isaiah, Proverbs, the Song of Songs, and Ecclesiastes."[3] Therefore, by the end of Hezekiah's reign the book of Proverbs had been compiled.

---

3. Babylonian Talmud, Tractate *Baba Batra* 15a (London: Soncino, 1935).

Whoever listens to me [wisdom] will live in safety
and be at ease, without fear of harm.

Proverbs 1:33

1

WISDOM AS THE GOAL (1:1-33)

Proverbs 1 reveals a number of goals for wisdom. Some of them are foundational and help us recognize the basis for wisdom. Other goals are quite practical. Through them, wisdom attempts to reach out and touch lives.

FOUNDATION (1:2-7)

WISDOM'S MOTTO (1:7)

The fear of the Lord is the beginning of knowledge (1:7a).
The fear of the Lord is the beginning of wisdom (9:10b).
The fear of the Lord teaches a man wisdom (15:33a).

These statements easily become the keynote of the whole book (also see chapter 8). Before we even start to take hold of wisdom we must recognize the one who has control of our lives and approach Him in faith and reverence. To fear the Lord does not mean to live in terror of the Lord, but neither is the phrase to be weakened by any lip service about awe or reverence that does not bring the heart into total submission to God.

The appropriate attitude of fear is best illustrated when Daniel (Daniel 10:8-10) and John (Revelation 1:17), confronted by the presence of God, fell on their faces before Him. In other words, there is no real beginning in the search for wisdom until there is first an acknowledgment of the one who has revealed Himself by His holy name (Exodus 3:13-15).

When we submit in worship to the Lord, we can begin to acquire knowledge. But this is not merely storing up scraps of information in the brain; rather, we enter into an intellectual and experiential knowledge designed to enable us to live in obedience to His will.

The second line of 1:7 ("fools despise wisdom and discipline") provides an *antithetic parallel* to "the fear of the Lord is the beginning of knowledge." Though the motto of Proverbs introduces the concepts of wisdom, knowledge, and discipline, we must first deal with the absolute necessity of a proper attitude requisite for enjoying these concepts. Those who reject this fear of the Lord and actually despise the wisdom that comes from Him are described as "foolish ones." The word picture for "fools" is the "thick-brained" and "stubborn ones." Therefore, anyone who turns up his nose at divine wisdom is unskilled in God's ways and offensively ignorant. He tends to become quarrelsome, mischievous, and lustful, having just the opposite attitudes and actions of the wise person who seeks to do the will of God (see chapter 11).

The relation between "the fear of the Lord" and true wisdom is that fear is the foundation and wisdom is the superstructure for moral and spiritual maturity. To be a completely whole person, one needs both of these qualities. Today's worldly-wise generation can calculate the path of a missile but cannot point the empty heart toward the path to the knowledge of God. We need more people today who can say with Solomon of old, "Give your servant a discerning heart" (1 Kings 3:9).

If the goal of life is wisdom, the question, "What is wisdom?" must be answered. Most people consider the acquisition of wisdom to be desirable, but they need a firm grasp of what it is they are seeking: "Hebrew Wisdom was practical, based on revealed principles of right and wrong, to be lived out in daily life."[1] Another way to think of wisdom is simply as "giving thought to your ways," which includes all aspects of life (physical, spiritual, financial, emotional, relational). In the book of Proverbs wisdom "enables the believer to know how to conduct himself toward other people and make the most of his spiritual opportunities."[2]

The term *wisdom* is the key word of the book. It is not speculation wherein people share their own philosophies of thought. Wisdom, as used in the Bible, refers to the knowledge of all good things and to a wide acquaintance with sound ethics in all learning. We shall examine the many qualities of wisdom when considering the benefits of wisdom, which enable a genuine moral and spiritual intelligence. God's wisdom is designed to give the child of God a knowledge enabling him or her to live life in its highest and best possible sense.

THE PURPOSE OF PROVERBS (1:5)

> Let the wise listen and add to their learning,
> and let the discerning get guidance (1:5).

Another suggested reading begins this verse with "A wise man will hear" (NASB*). The context, however, seems to suggest the grammatical structure of an exhortation that stops short of a direct command. Wisdom is not merely for the young and inexperienced. Rather, as young believers advance in the skill of hearing and doing, they are encouraged never to stop in this pursuit. In this life, no one comes to a certain point and feels that he has attained perfection. In fact, the exhortation of the second line says, "Let the wise add to [increase in] their learning [taking]." The wise person is expected to continue to enlarge on

* *New American Standard Bible*
1. R. Laird Harris, Gleason L. Archer, and Bruce K. Waltke, *Theological Wordbook of the Old Testament* (Chicago: Moody, 1980), 1:283.
2. Charles F. Pfeiffer, Howard F. Vos, and John Rea, *The Wycliffe Bible Encyclopedia* (Chicago: Moody, 1975), 2:1814.

what is his for the "taking." To mature in the Lord is to continually lay hold on what wisdom has to offer.

The purpose is further amplified when the wise one is described as a person with discernment who ought to get or "acquire [buy] wise counsels [pl]." The word picture for "wise counsels" is a nautical term referring to the roping used for steering the ancient wooden ships. Just as there is need for skill in steering these ships with all their sails, so there is need for the wise counsels of God that provide for skill and strategy in the management of life's difficult situations.

Note the effort involved in obtaining the wise counsels. The wise man is urged to get or buy this commodity. The means for exchange are not spelled out, but no doubt a high cost is involved to gain spiritual management skills. We have to realize that no advance in spiritual or wisdom stature is without a price paid in work, devotion, time, and, in some instances, money.

The exhortation to hear and increase in learning and the admonition to buy wise counsels at great cost need to be well understood. Coach Yost of the University of Michigan once had words with a football player who was overconfident enough to boast that Michigan's eleven would win simply because they had the will to win. The coach reminded the player that more important than the will to *win* was the will to *prepare*. This trainer had in mind the many hours on the field of practice, the tired bodies, and the fatigued minds. Only this kind of preparation could ensure victory. Are the purposes of Proverbs a part of *our* daily program? There is a price tag to gaining wisdom and becoming skillful in the ways of God.

THE BENEFITS OF WISDOM (1:2-4, 6)

Four benefits of studying wisdom are suggested by the book of Proverbs. These are described by means of five verbs: *attaining, understanding, acquiring, giving,* and, again, *understanding.* The many aspects of wisdom are pictured by the nouns or phrases: wisdom and discipline; words of insight; prudent life; right, just, and fair; prudence, knowledge, and discretion; proverbs and parables; and the sayings and riddles of the wise.

Attaining wisdom and discipline, understanding words of insight (1:2). The first verb of active involvement is "to attain," or "to know." Through it, one can obtain knowledge or wisdom. A believer has to have an informed mind to know intellectually and by experience the will and Word of God. The wise believer knows the Word and has personal experience in doing God's will. But "to know" in a biblical sense requires entering into a personal relationship with God Himself. Intellectual knowledge is necessary, but the need also exists for the *soul* to have communion with God. When the creature and Creator know each other, they have fellowship together and the creature lives in His will (1 John 1:6-7). With this kind of knowledge, the disciple is led into wisdom (see the discussion of 1:7).

An interesting quality of wisdom is "discipline," an important noun in Proverbs. To know this benefit is an experience in humility. The knowledge of God must include the possibility of God's teaching, correcting, and disciplining His disciple. This is the educational process Proverbs seeks to impart as foundational to the practice of self-discipline.

In still another benefit of active involvement, Proverbs enables individuals to understand "words of insight" (lit., "to discern the words of discernment"). The play on words is for a purpose. The peculiar meaning of "discern" is the ability to make proper moral distinctions. Here, the wise disciple can have the benefit of being able to distinguish the difference between good and evil speech, actions, and attitudes. These benefits of wisdom are for every believer who desires them.

The gift of insight (1:3). The benefits of Proverbs continue to increase. The wise disciple is to acquire "a disciplined and prudent life." *To acquire* describes another verb of active involvement with wisdom. To be able to acquire the many possibilities of wisdom is regarded as a distinct opportunity. To acquire (or to take) emphasizes an obligation that wisdom's possibilities are always present. The grace and graciousness of God enables His child to have every advantage to live the best kind of life.

The wise disciple acquires "a disciplined and prudent life." The word *disciplined* echoes the "discipline" of verse 2. It refers to "instruction," the peculiar educational process by which we can receive these benefits. But what are those specific benefits that God asks us to receive? Four kinds of wisdom are described by means of several nouns.

"The prudent life" means primarily "wise conduct." This is a quality defined by insight, good sense, and practical wisdom, dimensions so necessary for proper relations between people (3:4). At times, "wise conduct" can also have the further meaning of "success," not from a worldly point of view, but in the sense that the wise disciple will be well thought of and have spiritual blessings. David was so successful (very wise) that Saul was afraid of him (1 Samuel 18:15). Joshua also had this benefit as he meditated on the Word day and night (Joshua 1:8). We shall yet see many occurrences of this word in Proverbs.

Three additional features of godly wisdom are for "the taking" by the believer: doing what is right, just, and fair. To do what is *right* is that *correct relationship* between human beings that makes for the best possible social and moral contacts. By being *just* is meant the *application of righteousness* in affairs of judgment; no opportunity can be given for interfering with right decisions when making a judgment about the many encounters between people. To do what is *fair* is to be *straightforward* in conduct as opposed to the crooked ways of those who insist that they have no need for any guidance in moral truth and practice.

Note how these qualities occur in 2:9, Psalm 89:14, and Psalm 97:2; these three qualities are the bases upon which God's throne is established. Their combination is the natural outcome of the insight or wise behavior already mentioned. Far more acceptable to God than all the material blessings He could ever bestow is high regard and esteem for the gift of insight. Material gifts can be consumed by moths and rust or fall into the hands of those who do not appreciate all the hard work that went into acquiring these gifts. The gift of insight, or wise behavior, has eternal value and consequence.

The immature can be invulnerable (1:4). The gem-studded display of benefits continues to grow. We note the generous benefactor of these gifts: "giving," or "He gives." Previously, the disciples were encouraged to receive (1:3), but now the attention is centered on the one involved in giving.

He gives to "the simple" or naive (lit., "open ones"). The open-minded ones are sometimes described as simple ones, but certainly not in any questionable sense. These are the immature who are open to influence, whether good or evil. They are not yet set in any particular way of life; the object of particular attention is the young person. In a special sense, the new believer can also be included as well, no matter what the age.

God offers such people, who have not come to well-defined moral and spiritual decisions, a specific kind of wisdom: "the prudent life," or "shrewdness." The sage does not have the wrong kind of craftiness in mind. Rather, the stress is that, with right planning and decision-making, a person can guard himself against being led astray. Jesus Christ Himself used this concept when He exhorted guileless disciples to be shrewd as snakes (not easily fooled) but also innocent (simple or harmless) as doves (Matthew 10:16).

The second line of 1:4 reflects a synonymous parallel with line one: the young person is likened to the "open-minded" or person of tender age, generally the teenager who is inexperienced in the ways of the world. To such is given by God the possibility of wisdom in its different aspects, in particular knowledge (see the discussion of 1:2).

In addition, discretion is offered. The young person can, literally, have the "power to purpose," to decide wisely, when making honorable decisions. Wisdom offers the best possible counsel to help the teenager avoid the fraud and falsehood of the world as he or she launches out into life.

Perhaps the best illustration of having these benefits of prudence (shrewdness) and discretion in the positive sense is that the "prudent man sees danger and takes refuge, but the simple keep going and suffer for it" (22:3). With shrewdness and discretion, the wise young disciple can avoid those pitfalls in the world that would rob him of living the best possible kind of life. The immature and inexperienced need not be vulnerable.

Spiritual discernment (1:6). We come to the climax of a series of benefits of wisdom for the disciple. How different and strange are such blessings to people of the world geared to the attainment of wealth, power, position, and immortality. Contrary to this, wisdom offers a distinctive level of achievement: "understanding" or "to understand" (lit., "discern"). For one to discern implies maturity in making distinctions. Every child of God is encouraged to reach this goal. But what shall one discern as the goal and climax of wisdom and its various parts?

First, one should discern "proverbs," that is, their nature (see Introduction). The believer in the school of wisdom has the obligation to advance in wisdom, grasping the meaning of likenesses and resemblances, which refer to the crisp, pungent, common-sense advice in correct morals provided by the proverbs.

Second, the believer must also learn to discern the interpretation of "parables." There are several basic meanings for this term, but the idea behind the Hebrew for "parables" here is the taunt by or the scorn of the wise teacher toward his disciples. And yet the disciple must develop in maturity so that he can appropriate for himself these remarks, which are designed to correct. He should not feel offended when a taunt is hurled at him; the scornful remark is designed for his own good. In these kinds of situations we sometimes learn our best lessons.

"The sayings of the wise" must also be carefully measured. Men and women who are advanced in the grace and knowledge of God's ways and who have demonstrated these lessons in their lives should be carefully observed.

Their precepts are to be received as an example for godly living by the young believer.

Finally, the disciple is to discern "riddles" or "enigmas," the dark obscure sayings already pictured in the wardrobe of wisdom (see Introduction). These riddles are to be studied and diligently grasped because they are moral truths couched in language that provokes thought and issues a challenge. Sometimes a truth expressed in such a way is never forgotten. The benefits of wisdom prompt us to ask ourselves, What comes *first* in our lives, the things of the world or the epitome of God's wisdom?

PRACTICAL OUTREACH (1:8-33)

Wisdom has much to say regarding practical applications of her teaching: the importance of good parenting, the dangers of the "easy life," and the paramount importance of heeding wisdom's appeals.

PARENTAL EXHORTATIONS (1:8-9)

As the teacher speaks to his disciples, the master combines and balances his command to "listen" with the endearing term "my son." Proper instruction always needs to combine love and discipline. The dearly beloved pupil is to listen diligently to his teacher's lessons and then put into practice what he hears. Before anything else is said, the student is reminded of his parental exhortations. Wisdom places great importance upon the role of the family unit and ultimate value upon parental instruction.

The father's responsibility is *to instruct his children*, and, as previously mentioned, the Hebrew word for *instruction* is the more stern one used in verse 3: "a disciplined life." This may sound harsh, but as this instruction administered by the father is coupled with a humble submission by the young person to obey, the child will learn to someday discipline himself or herself without parental intervention.

The mother's part is *teaching*, or giving direction and guidance. The mother seems to be the one who provides oral exhortations; thus, her share in the family unit would be of a gentler nature. In fact, the literal meaning of her training is, "Do not even begin to forsake the teaching of your mother." If the child should try it, the father will hear about it.

Many people in the Middle East wore beautiful adornments on the head, as well as ornamental necklaces (Genesis 41:42). Parents gave these as gifts to their children, and a great deal of sentiment was attached to them. Just as these ornaments were intended for adornment, as well as a reminder of loving parents, so also were the instructions of a father and the teaching of a mother to be highly regarded. Loving obedience to parental exhortations was designed by God to give grace and dignity in the life of every son and daughter. By following parental advice, children and young people could grow and mature and eventually achieve the maximum that life can offer in the adult years.

"Honor your father and your mother" says the fifth commandment (Exodus 20:12). Because this word was among the first five commandments, with their emphasis on what God desires, parents are reminded they are His representatives to guide their children in godly living. Children are, therefore, to honor their parents, but the latter are held responsible for their role in child training.

ALLURE OF THE "EASY LIFE" (1:10-14)

Another goal of wisdom is to remind the young person of the many dangers in succumbing to the temptations of easy living. Those who are in their teens or early twenties are warned of the concept of "something for nothing." Temptations are bound to come: "sinners entice you [or, lure you by opening a way]" (1:10). As long as there is a world of people in bondage to sin, the ungodly will persuade the gullible by means of alluring but empty promises. These sinners have a way of flattery (or enticement), but their hearts are not right (Psalm 78:36-37).

What is the *bait* dangled by these sinners? The offer is for worldly gain of money and goods without working for it. "Come along with us," they say, "let us grab." The *offer* is for valuable things (1:13) and plunder. The allure is for the short, quick route to success in the world. The argument is that the person who has the wealth of this world can command respect and wield power.

The *basis* for the easy life is robbery. Wealth is to be stolen, and the houses of the sinners are to be filled with spoil (1:13). Unsuspecting and unarmed folk are to be ambushed; people who have not harmed these sinners in any way are to be trapped (1:11). Easy robbery is in mind, since innocent people's possessions are to be grabbed before they realize what had happened.

But the *means* of easy living is violence and murder. If innocent victims attempt to defend themselves, their blood will be shed and they will suffer death (1:11-12). The goal of the easy life justifies every violent assault upon human dignity.

The *decision* to pursue the easy life is to actively respond to the challenge "come along with us," "join up with us," "we will share a common purse" (1:11, 14). The innocent beginner is tempted to be an equal partner right from the start. His ego is flattered, making it easy for him to decide to join in the fun.

What is the loving teacher's advice concerning these allures? He begins with the endearing term "my son," and then immediately points out the moral evil of such activity. He emphatically insists that the people who do these things are "sinners" (1:10). Then he abruptly breaks off and says sharply, "Do not give in," or, literally, "Do not even begin to go." The easy life can only end in a lost eternity with nothing to show for such an abominable "easy" effort.

A WARNING AGAINST THE "EASY LIFE" (1:15-19)

The wise teacher is not finished with this easy life, and he carefully warns the immature and inexperienced who might find attractive the philosophy of something for nothing. In a wise, clever manner, the teacher describes the sinful ways of these wicked people who prey on their fellow human beings and points out the miserable end of those involved in this easy living.

"Let me show you what will happen to them," says the sage, as he launches into a description of how certain birds are captured. Grain scattered out on the ground in a specific area attracts unsuspecting birds, and they swoop down on the desirable morsel of food. But these creatures do not realize that a net was previously spread out under the food. As soon as the birds start to eat, the net is swiftly pulled tight. By then it is too late, and the birds are at the mercy of their captors.

In just the same way will these "something for nothing" fellows fall into a trap. They think they have the power to shed blood indefinitely and to pounce on unsuspecting people without end. But in the long run, the kind of life these sinners have led will collapse in disaster. Suddenly, unexpectedly, their lives will come to an end.

Those who "go after ill-gotten gain" (lit., "plunderers of plunder") will one day have the trap sprung on them (1:19). As the bird flutters its wings helplessly in a secure trap, so one day these plunderers will be caught, and no mercy will be extended to them.

The teacher now issues his warning. Speaking in terms of endearment, but also with authority, he says, literally, "My son, do not even begin to walk in the way with them" (cf. 1:15a). He actually raises his voice in command: "Do not set [or, refuse your] foot on their paths [or, course of life]" (1:15b). The wise teacher's desire for his young students and disciples is that they stay clear of the "gang," the companions who continually live evil lives.

THE SHOUT BY WISDOM (1:20-23)

Wisdom now actively pursues her goal. Personified as a woman, she walks out into the broad stream of life to attract people to herself. The word for wisdom here is in the plural (as in 9:1; 24:7). This is for the purpose of expressing her intensity and the fullness of her search and offer. She seeks to reach the multitudes in the areas where people congregate, particularly the simple or naive folk.

The *presence* of wisdom is seen in public. She does not confine herself merely to the special few in search of knowledge; rather, she is in the streets among the crowds, in the public squares where she raises her voice to be heard (1:20). She cries out at the head, or chief area, of streets made noisy by the bazaars and marketplaces (1:21). Wisdom is an outdoors preacher. Many of the prophets ministered in these familiar places, where the teeming masses were located (Isaiah 22:2; Lamentations 2:19).

Wisdom also makes her speech in the gates of the walls, where the city officials sat to judge local matters. Therefore, like the merchants who brought their goods to the crowded cities to find customers for their wares, wisdom offers her benefits to as many as will listen and make the effort to receive her.

The *preaching* of wisdom is an appeal in the form of heart-searching questions: "How long will you simple ones love your simple ways?" (1:22). The word "simple," or naive, is the same as in 1:4—"open ones"—except now it refers to those who open themselves up to ignorance. The message continues: "How long will mockers delight in mockery" and "fools . . . hate [make a habit of hating] knowledge." The implied question is, "How long will you continue to make a habit of this life-style?"

Wisdom points out the steady downward slide of people who will not listen to her ethical advice: beginning with the simple (immature), they digress to become mockers and end up, finally, as fools. What a sad commentary on what happens to people in the period from childhood to adulthood when they do not turn to the Lord. But no one will ever be able to fault wisdom. She persists in her tasks, issuing a direct command to listen and repent (or turn around) from a wrong way of life—"If you had responded [lit., turned] to my rebuke" (1:23a).

The *present* of wisdom is a stupendous offer: "I would have poured out my heart to [lit., my spirit on] you and made my thoughts [lit., words] known to you" (1:23b-c). The verb "poured out" is the same root word used when God caused the prophet "to bubble or gush forth" with the Word of God. Wisdom does likewise to whoever desires this gracious gift. We can then know and experience the thoughts and words that come from God Himself. The goal of wisdom is to reach people and establish them in the family of God. May our prayer be, "All our lives, O Lord, help us as believers to yield to wisdom's call."

WISDOM'S SECURITY AND THE FOOL'S SCORN (1:24-33)

Wisdom has called to the multitudes on life's pathway (1:22-23), and many are the folk who do respond and find God's blessing in their lives and souls. But, tragically, what do the multitudes of the simple ones, mockers, and fools do with the earnest pleas of wisdom for their own good?

The fool's *reaction* to wisdom's pleas is largely a refusal to have anything to do with her. Her outstretched hand with an offer of gain can actually provoke an outright refusal, with "no one" giving "heed" (1:24). Wisdom's advice or rebuke is "ignored" (1:25*a*).

But this reaction is not necessarily passive; sinners can actually become antagonistic. The multitudes, then as now, can "hate knowledge" (see 1:22*c*; 1:29*a*) and "not choose to fear the Lord" (1:29*b*). People have a way of despising and "spurning" any correction (1:30*b*). What a picture of the human heart sinking down to the depths of sin. How the beautiful woman, wisdom, has been stained and made dirty by sinful men in their choices and deeds.

The *reproof* by wisdom is sharp. She is not helpless by any means. The day is coming when calamity will strike. The time is soon coming for those events in life that fill people's hearts with terror. "Disaster," "calamity," "distress and troubles" will all too quickly be the portion of those who laugh at and despise wisdom (1:26-27). When life's troubles come to those who have spurned wisdom, she will "laugh" and "mock" in turn.

These mockers and fools will one day seek help and cry diligently for release from their misfortunes, but God "will not answer" to undo the consequences of sin (1:28*a*). Does this sound harsh? Yet the main emphasis of the lesson is the bitter pill of living as a fool. The person who makes a habit of this life-style becomes hardened through continually making wrong choices. The teacher's lesson is a forceful reproof of the foolishness of choosing a life of sin.

The *retribution* of rejecting wisdom will be full and final (1:30-32). No truly repentant sinner ever seeks God and wisdom in vain (1:33). His promise to the one who has listened to wisdom is that he or she "will live in safety and be at ease, without fear of harm" (1:33). But the people who make a habit of continually rejecting wisdom and her God will begin to "eat the fruit of their ways" (1:31). The New Testament sequel is that "a man reaps what he sows" (Galatians 6:7). The final step in rebelliousness, apostasy, and careless ease is destruction. What a fearful price to pay for the complete rejection of the gracious appeal by wisdom. Scorn or mockery, security or peace—the choice is ours.

For the Lord gives wisdom,
and from his mouth come knowledge and understanding.

Proverbs 2:6

2

THE FRUITS OF WISDOM (2:1-22)

We became acquainted with some of the characteristics of wisdom in the Introduction and the goals and aims of wisdom in chapter 1. Now we turn to the fruits of learning wisdom. The sages sought to elicit a responsive chord in people's hearts by teaching wisdom. But for what purpose?

Basic, of course, was that people should know the Lord. Then, as believers were further discipled in the many dimensions of wisdom, certain desirable moral and spiritual traits were the result. No wonder the believer in the Old Testament was referred to many times as "the righteous man" who took no pride in self-righteousness. The emphasis was placed on the *results* of what happens to a properly disciplined believer.

WISDOM PRESENTS HER CONDITIONS (2:1-4)

To have the fruits of wisdom, the disciple must recognize and meet the conditions set by wisdom. The ways of God are simple, but the seeker needs to sense how God operates. His promises can be ours at any time, but certain conditions must be met before His word can be fulfilled. First, He tells us to "trust," "lean not," and "ac-

41

knowledge" (3:5-6a); when we meet these conditions of faith, His promise is to "make [our] paths straight" (3:6a). The second condition concerns prayer: we must call upon the Lord. When we do, His promise is that we will experience "great and unsearchable things [we] do not know" (Jeremiah 33:3).

Just as the prophet spoke in the name of God, so the teacher, as a personification of God, speaks out in the name of wisdom (see Introduction). The sage lays down conditions the disciple must meet, and when the pupil in the school of wisdom meets them, he can expect the blessings of wisdom in his life. What, then, are the conditions that must be met by the young person who desires wisdom?

The young person is told to "accept" or "take hold" of the teacher's words (2:1a). If he would be wise, the disciple will not let one word slip away. The reference to "commands" (commandments) relates to rules of proper moral conduct that have been derived from observation and experience and are in conformity with the Bible. Just as the pupil "accepts" the teacher's word, so he is expected to "store up" these commands until they become a part of him (2:1b).

The young person listens by "turning" his ear to wisdom (2:2a). (See the Introduction for the meaning of wisdom as the sum total of all moral and spiritual intelligence.) The heart, regarded as the seat of man's intellect and emotions, includes all human desires, thoughts, conceptions, and will. The supreme desire by wisdom is for her disciple to apply his or her "heart to understanding [or, discernment]" (2:2b). (See the discussion on discernment at 1:2 in chapter 1.)

As if to emphasize sharply what is to follow, 2:3 is introduced by a strong break ("and"), which is meant to strongly encourage the pursuits in 2:3-4 to meet wisdom's conditions. The young person is to "call out" for the gift of "insight," or discriminatory judgment (2:3a). Should he not be heard, the pupil is to "cry aloud," again and again if need be, to attain "understanding," or discernment (2:3b). Just as prayer necessitates a continual asking, seeking, and knocking (Matthew 7:7), so discernment only comes with diligent search.

A person must "look" for wisdom as he would carefully prospect for silver ore (2:4a). In fact, the prevalent custom was to hide precious valuables in the ground (Isaiah 45:3; Jeremiah 41:8), and when these were needed, people very carefully and diligently dug them up. Wisdom is to be sought after in this fashion.

On this matter of meeting conditions for attaining wisdom, note the ever increasing intensity of the verbs and the added meaningfulness of the nouns. Every disciple has to proceed from *accepting words* and *storing up commandments* to *searching earnestly* (digging energetically) for wisdom and discernment as if he were searching for the most valuable of "hidden treasure."

We are impressed by a seeming contradiction. In 1:20-23, wisdom calls for adherents and offers them the free gift of herself and her spirit. In 2:1-4 the *disciple* has to call diligently for wisdom and her gifts. The parallel is the free offer of salvation to whosoever will come. But once a person knows the Lord, the advance in spirituality and morality may have a high price tag, taking everything one has in the commitment of time and resources. So it is with believers as they relate to wisdom. From the time we accept Jesus as Savior, we have to continually meet the conditions laid down by wisdom in order to mature into strong believers.

WISDOM REVEALS GOD (2:5-11)

The proper regard for wisdom and of her reception leads to an encounter with God that not only includes reverential awe but also intimate experience. These two experiences seem to be opposites. How does one stand in awe before a holy God and yet be intimate with Him? How can one fellowship with God and have respect for His holiness? Yet wisdom makes this possible as another of her fruits.

We can "understand [or, discern] the fear of the Lord" (2:5a). The wisdom of the Word will help us to recognize, to a limited degree, the awesomeness of the very being of God. If we do not begin to perceive His sovereignty and separateness, which drives us to our knees before Him, we will also never have right views of our obligations to Him or be able to enjoy His mercy and grace. But along with respect for the fear of the Lord is the possibility to "find the knowledge of God" (2:5b) so that we can have communion of soul with Him. We can have fellowship with the Lord as friend with friend. All of these offers imply, by their very nature, a new heart experience for the disciple.

When we accept the wisdom of the Word, we enter into a new kind of life never known before. We find that the Lord is in the habit of providing wisdom, for He is its source (2:6a). From God's mouth comes an intimate "knowledge" of Him as well as "understanding" or discrimination in judgment (2:6b). The "upright" ones, walking in the light of the Word, have "victory in store" in all their pursuits (2:7a). The last phrase can also mean "sound wisdom" and is a word occurring often in Proverbs and Job. Its many occurrences suggest that the disciple has a grasp on sound spiritual and moral truth and that he or she can apply this kind of wisdom to everyday affairs of life with God's full approval.

God Himself becomes "a shield [or, an aid] to those whose walk is blameless" (2:7a). Literally, "blameless" is "wholeness, completeness," indicating the well-rounded moral life. God is pictured as a military officer who "guards the course of the just and protects the way of his faithful ones" (2:8). The folk for whom He has special regard love Him and are loved by Him (2:8).

Words of wisdom reveal God to us so that we can have fellowship with Him, and as we enjoy this fellowship, we experience an even greater outpouring of wisdom (2:9-11). The paradox is very much in evidence; the more we receive the wisdom of God in His words, the more is revealed to us about God. There is no end to this process except when we break the cycle and make wrong choices in life.

The child of God can "understand," or discern, what is right and just and fair. Indeed, on every path of goodness, he can enjoy the blessings of wisdom in everyday life (2:9). "Wisdom will enter" the heart of the totally committed disciple to guide in all moral affairs. The knowledge he or she derives from this communion with God "will be pleasant to [the] soul" (2:10).

Discretion, or the taunt designed to correct (see discussion of 1:4), is the means used by wisdom to guard the disciple (2:11a). So will wisdom's gracious offer of "understanding [or, discriminating judgment] . . . guard" every child of God (2:11b). Biblical wisdom reveals God and provides its fruits for the maturing of the disciple.

WISDOM "SIZES" PEOPLE (2:12-22)

Wisdom has a way of "fitting" people according to size much as we use certain measures to fit our suits, dresses, and shoes. Since wisdom here is a biblical wisdom that reflects an absolute standard, the fit will always be an accurate one. Wisdom takes a careful look at people and shows why some people will never partake of her fruits.

EVIL MEN (2:12-15)

Wisdom sizes the "words" and interests of evil men (2:12-15). The first measurement is applied to those "whose words are perverse [lit., upside down]" (2:12b). The expression alludes to those who would turn the Word of God upside down to make it evil, seeking at the same time to justify their wicked words and teaching. Another accurate fit is that these evil men "leave the straight paths to walk in dark ways" (2:13). Proverbs describes the ways of evil people as always engulfed in blackness, while by contrast the upright have paths flooded with light.

Wisdom portrays wicked men as those who take "delight in doing wrong" and who actually "rejoice in the perverseness of evil" (2:14). Do these people choose evil ways because they do not know any better? Hardly. For people to speak of that which is morally upside down and then to rejoice in these thoughts and actions only proves that they have *chosen* what they want for their happiness.

This only compounds the sentence of judgment by God. From wisdom's view, the choices for evil were deliberate, and these men are guilty because they stand against God's Word and His ways (note also Isaiah 5:20-21).

How does wisdom point out the way by which choices should be made? Simply this: Wicked men rejoice in their choices for evil, while godly people sorrow over their sins.

Is it any wonder that, in the final sizing, these sinful characters are described as those who walk in paths that are "crooked and who are devious in their ways" (2:15)? Their morals are twisted. They are "devious," which means that they turn away from anything godly. These wicked men who persist in their ways will someday have to acknowledge that wisdom made no mistake in sizing them correctly as to their character analysis.

The child of God is warned about these sinful people. Wisdom's disciples are encouraged instead to taste of the fruits of wisdom. They are to take delight in the knowledge of communion with God and cultivate abiding wisdom in the heart (2:10). When this is so, the talk, attitudes, and actions of evil men will be foreign to them; the fruits of wickedness will be considered part of an alien world. God offers wisdom and knowledge to deliver a person from being sized with wicked folk. Better it is to be sized as a godly person than as an evil one.

THE ADULTEROUS WOMAN (2:16-22)

Wisdom is not through with the lesson of fitting evil people in garments that match their wickedness. Now, she singles out a special case: the adulterous woman. Wisdom dresses her in the garments of "seductive words" (2:16b), which can only adorn her for ultimate doom and destruction. This is certainly no fruit of wisdom. Satan instead offers such foolishness to the unsuspecting and immature person.

The expression used for "adulteress," or strange woman, refers to a non-Israelite woman (a woman of the outside). The context, however, deals with immorality, and so "outside," in this case, refers to the Israelite woman seeking satisfaction apart from her own family circle. In so doing, she is regarded as disgusting. But this state of affairs can apply to any society, not just the society of ancient Israel.

The first measurement, in wisdom's eyes, is a soiled garment. Here, and in several other passages to be considered later, immorality is ultimately pictured as attractive but also deplorable. The child of God is to be warned: the clothes of immorality are considered dirty.

The adulterous (or strange) woman is described as choosing her words so well that they are extremely enticing and "seductive" (2:16b). One can almost see the coy wink of the eye that goes with the smooth speech.

The fitting continues as this woman is charged with leaving the "partner" (leader or lord) of her youth (2:17a). The expression alludes to her husband. Notice the same expression and meaning in Jeremiah 3:4, where God is regarded as the husband of Israel, with the nation itself as the wife.

In the synthetic parallel statement, the immoral woman "has . . . ignored [or, is unmindful of] the covenant she made before God" (2:17b), by which her marriage tie to her husband was recognized. Not even a mere passing sexual encounter between a man and woman was acceptable because the Word of God prohibited adultery (Exodus 20:13). God is the witness in a wedding ceremony where the husband and wife promise to be faithful to each other. When the marriage covenant is broken, such immorality becomes an insult to God.

The consequences of this sizing are given in repulsive language to make potential offenders think twice before yielding to temptation. The warning, directed toward both sexes, is to never even consider adultery.

The house of the adulteress is described as a place of pleasure and sensual delights; in actuality it is a trap for those who indulge outside the moral bounds. Her house becomes synonymous with death (2:18-19, 22). The participants in immorality go "down to death" and are on the "paths to the spirits of the dead" (2:18). In the Old Testament, *sheol* was the destination of the departed ones, both saved and unsaved, and there was an uncrossable chasm between these two groups of people (see the comment by Abraham in Luke 16:26). Wisdom points out that a person who continually practices immorality will go out of this world as an unbeliever to *sheol*. Such a life-style only invites physical disaster and eternal suffering. Once in *sheol*, no return to life for another opportunity is possible.

The young man and the young woman are to mark this "size" well and not be enticed. Such a course of life is not what God intends for anyone. Sad to say, multitudes follow in pursuit of this woman, but her offer of pleasure is soiled clothing, in contrast to the shining, clean garments of wisdom. Wisdom's offer enables the believer to find the company of "the upright" and enjoy God's favor and blessings (2:21).

The wider application today is that our choices are sharp and clear. There are no shades of gray. Wisdom offers her fruits, and her disciples must consider immorality as off limits. Wisdom's pupils must understand the moral absolutes God has laid down and intend with their entire heart to follow them.

She [wisdom] is a tree of life to those who embrace her;
those who lay hold of her will be blessed.

Proverbs 3:18

3

THE WISE DISCIPLE (3:1-35)

Paul the apostle once asked, "Where is the wise man? Where is the scholar? Where is the philosopher of this age? Has not God made foolish the wisdom of the world?" (1 Corinthians 1:20). In context, the apostle demonstrates that, if the wisdom of the world has no guidance from the wisdom of God, then man's wisdom stands apart from God and is, in reality, foolishness. All truth is of God and is shared in common with all people, both believers and unbelievers. People are created in the image of God and possess, more or less, an appreciation for truth. But how is this truth applied? Unsaved and ungodly people, because of their sin nature, can pervert truth for their own purpose. Tragically, they turn away; for their thinking becomes futile, and their foolish hearts are darkened (Romans 1:21).

For the disciple who would be wise in God's ways wisdom comes and provides for a proper application of truth, which will honor the Lord and make possible untold blessings. There is no limit to this wisdom and what she can offer; she is never stingy with her gifts but, rather, will give and give without end. No wonder Paul exclaimed, "Oh, the depth of the riches of the wisdom and knowledge of God! How unsearchable his judgments, and his paths beyond tracing out!" (Romans 11:33). The third chapter of Proverbs primarily points out the potential for blessings for every wise disciple. We begin with 3:5-6, which is really the heart of the discussion and then see how the truth of this text works itself out in the rest of the passage.

The Sanctuary of the Soul (3:5-6)

Psalm 23 is known as the shepherd's psalm. Just as the sheep are utterly dependent upon their shepherd, so the child of God must repose in the leadership of the Great Shepherd and find his soul's sanctuary in the Lord. In perhaps the best known passage in Proverbs, wisdom emphasizes the sanctuary of the soul.

A sanctuary is found by *trusting* in the Lord (3:5a), and the main idea behind the word *trust* is "to cling to" or "lean upon." The wise disciple is the one who, having received a word from the Lord, accepts it and acts upon it as true. He leans hard upon God; He has cast all his hopes for the present and future upon Him.

Furthermore, this trust must be an experience with the whole heart, one that is completely undivided. The first commandment defines this singleness of purpose: "Love the Lord your God with all your heart and with all your soul and with all your strength" (Deuteronomy 6:5). This is a life-style for *all times*, both good or bad. We find it easy to trust when the sun is shining and everything is going well. But this is all the more reason to lean hard upon the Lord when the circumstances seem to be against us. The wise disciple is to be encouraged that in the storms of life he can have his greatest experience of God's all sufficiency.

A further sanctuary is found when we "lean not on [our] own understanding" (3:5b). Literally, the phrase is rendered: "Do not even begin to rely upon your own discrimination in judgment." We are so constituted that we often follow our plans and decisions based on the way we want to apply truth, even as believers. We learn many times to our dismay that our reasoning is fallible. We must have guidance by biblical wisdom to live completely within the will of God. Granted, learning to lean solely upon the Lord is a difficult lesson, but once learned nothing else brings complete rest to the soul.

The next verse commands that as we pursue life's activities we are to "acknowledge him," literally, "have a knowledge of Him or know Him" (3:6a). This is the knowledge of the heart's communion with God but not only for the times when we are alone with God. As we move about in our various circles of life, we are to always have Him in mind, so that by word and deed we become His testimonies in the world. Believers, therefore, serve as representatives of God, permeating a society caught up with atheism, secular humanism, immorality, scientific pursuits, and so on. But in addition, spiritual and wise believers can encourage other believers who are prone to be "practical atheists," making their choices as if God does not exist. Too often the latter is true, but godly believers can be a tower of strength to disciples who are floundering in their Christian testimony.

When we take these instructions to heart concerning the sanctuary of our souls, God now has a sure promise. For emphasis, the wise teacher literally says of God, "He—He will begin to make straight your paths" (3:6b). After the wise disciple meets wisdom's conditions, God removes all obstacles and helps him or her to properly walk on the path of life. Can a better sanctuary of the soul ever be found?

EXERCISING A VITAL FAITH (3:1-4, 7-8)

When God becomes the sanctuary of the disciple's soul, the exercise of a vital, living faith is made feasible. But for faith to be valid, it must be involved with the whole of life, in the positive as well as the negative choices.

Once more we see where the teacher has a loving concern for his charges when he says, "My son" (3:1). With this term of endearment, he wants his pupils to grasp the essentials that lead to life's best. It is necessary also that disciples sense the love of their teachers as a factor necessary for their encouragement.

With a proper balance of love and discipline (see discussion at 1:10), the teacher declares: "Do not" even beginto "forget [or, disregard] my teaching [lit., my law]" (3:1*a*). One may question whether a believer will actually "forget" a moral or spiritual truth. But the very real danger is that he or she will choose to ignore the everyday choices for good.

The teacher also reminds his students, and us as well, that the heart must "keep" (guard, watch over) God's commands that relate to our conduct (3:1*b*). No one can come to God and then try to live a faith-life apart from the Word; the truths of Scripture are what will enable us to live a vital faith, "prolong" our lives for "many years and bring . . . prosperity [or, peace]" (3:2). Though there may be exceptions, the statement is a general truth.

The teacher is also concerned with the deeds of faith. He adds, "Do not" even begin to "let love and faithfulness [or, truth] . . . leave [or, forsake] you" (3:3*a*). "Faith by itself, if it is not accompanied by action, is dead" (James 2:17), and when we demonstrate evidences of the supernatural in our lives, a vital faith will lead us to be doers of the Word. Positively, the works of loving-kindness and truth are to be a vital part of our life's fabric, bound as the ornament around the "neck" and written on "the tablet of our heart" (3:3*b-c*). Paul aptly applied the truth of this verse in a New Testament context: "Be kind and compassionate to one another, forgiving each other, just as in Christ God forgave you" (Ephesians 4:32).

The teacher again repeats the familiar refrain "Fear the Lord" (3:7*b*), which is the basic essential to gain the wisdom and knowledge of God. There is a negative side and meaning to the admonition. To know the objective of divine wisdom, the disciple is told, "Do not" even begin to "be wise in your own eyes" (chapter 3:7*a*). The misuse of God's truth and the vanity of human speculation is a barrier to the attainment of the wisdom of God.

We are also to "shun evil." We cannot avoid the wicked thoughts that pop into our heads, but indulgence in them and the consequence of the practice of evil lead one to be wise in his own sight, another upside-down set of moral choices. These are conditions by which one will never be led to fear the Lord. The disciple is thereby warned of what he has to avoid if he desires a right approach to God.

In the life of active faith, there can be the "health of holiness," or as wisdom described it, the possession of "prosperity" or peace, physical "health," and "nourishment to [the] bones" (3:2b, 8). Today, doctors know that a godly life and good physical health are often related: sexual morality, moderation in all things, and a contented life can prevent many ailments and diseases. A person in right relationship with God has the promise of inner peace through wisdom (3:2b) and, therefore, can enjoy a sense of calm and serenity within the soul. A joyful holiness is a healthy holiness in the exercise of a vital faith.

MATERIAL AND SPIRITUAL BLESSINGS (3:9-10)

This portion of Scripture had special meaning to all Israel under the Mosaic covenant, especially to the believer. If an Israeli farmer wanted his barns filled and his vats overflowing with the fruit of the vine, he had to learn that there was a definite connection between material blessings and his worship of the Lord. Obviously, if the farmer was a believer, he would have a particular sensitivity to honor the Lord with his wealth; he would present the first fruits from his produce and set aside special gifts for the work of God's servants. But when this sensitivity to the Lord's things was lacking, when believers drifted away from the Lord and the people became rebellious, drought came upon the land as judgment (Deuteronomy 28:1-19). God withheld the rain as a reminder that everyone should once more seek their God.

The emphasis on material things appears as an inducement on the lowest possible level. Jesus also may have felt this way: "Do not store up for yourselves treasures on earth . . . but store up for yourselves treasures in heaven" (Matthew 6:19-20). But the Mosaic covenant was a schoolmaster, providing instructions in how to know the Lord and how to appropriate every possible blessing. The Old Testament believer certainly knew the possibilities of loving the Lord, walking "in all his ways," and serving the Lord with all of the heart and soul (Deuteronomy 10:12). When he came to this stage in his experience, he could appreciate all the more the highest incentive that would lead him to have intimate fellowship with a loving Father. In turn, he could enjoy all spiritual and material blessings (Exodus 19:4-6; Leviticus 26:3-13; Deuteronomy 28:1-14). Likewise, the highest inducement for service in the New Testament was suggested by Paul when he declared: "Christ's love compels us" that we should no longer live for ourselves but for Him who died for us and was raised for us (2 Corinthians 5:14-15).

Of course there were exceptions to the general rule that material blessings were possible when people were obedient to the Lord. Many specific instances do mark material reverses in spite of saintly lives. For example, the musician Asaph struggled with questions about why the wicked prosper (Psalm 73:1-12); Naboth was treacherously put to death and his vineyard taken from him through the schemes of wicked queen Jezebel (1 Kings 21:5-13). But in such situations God was accomplishing particular purposes in individual lives. As a general rule the combination of great spiritual and material blessings reflected the divine purpose that Israel be a witness in the Middle East and attract interested individuals from pagan nations to know and worship the God of Israel.

The New Covenant does not have such an intricate relationship of spiritual and material blessings. The wise believer today can expect all *spiritual* blessings as he seeks to appropriate them (Ephesians 1:3). He does *not* specifically have a New Testament promise of material wealth, only that God will provide for all of his needs (Philippians 4:19). If there are riches, it is only because of God's sovereign will and pleasure. Not to have material wealth is no sign of God's displeasure. In fact, some of God's happiest and most fruitful saints have had very little of this world's goods.

Some preachers today insist that the believer can have material wealth if he claims it in prayer and then works hard for it.[1] Supposedly, God will then bless His child both materially and spiritually. This line of reasoning is faulty on two counts.

First, if the attempt is made to appropriate Old Testament truth along this line, the preacher is misinterpreting Scripture. Israel was constituted as a nation in the midst of a sea of pagan nations, and God had certain purposes to accomplish with and through them. Material wealth was one way to attract the interest of the pagans; therefore, the Lord blessed Israel that unbelievers of other nations might inquire about the God of this favored people. The Body of Christ is not a nation; instead, it consists of individual peoples from many nations. The universal Body on earth is an organism, not an organization, and each believer must be obedient to the laws of the country wherein he or she resides. God does not deal with the church on the same basis as Israel.

Second, the Bible contains no promise of material blessings for the church. Believers living in North America in a context of political freedom enjoy material prosperity, not because there is a covenant that promises it but because God has been merciful and gracious to the peoples of the United States and Canada. Japan also is prosperous, yet has an extremely small percentage of Christians. In contrast, godly believers in many other parts of the world have very little material goods. In fact, most believers in the Body of Christ in poor third-world countries know very well that God provides for bare needs and not much else. In nations such as the Soviet Union, believers have very little, but they live joyfully. We should, therefore, avoid misappropriating Old Testament truths not present in the New Testament and thereby mislead people and pervert their faith.

1. See Michael Horton, ed., *The Agony of Deceit: What Some TV Preachers Are Really Teaching* (Chicago: Moody, 1990); Bruce Barron, *The Health and Wealth Gospel: A Fresh Look at Healing, Prosperity & Positive Confession* (Downers Grove, Ill.: InterVarsity, 1987).

Furthermore, even the Old Testament believer, as he grew in grace, put more emphasis on areas other than material prosperity (see 3:13-15). Materialism can blind people and even lead believers astray. Rather, God had something better for the soul and spirit. So the end result is still the same for either the Old or New Testament believer: he or she can expect *spiritual* blessings for the practice of piety.

THE DISCIPLINE OF GOD (3:11-12)

The question, "Why?" has always been perplexing, even for a child of God. Job pondered it in the depths of his illness; Jeremiah uttered it in his despondency, when he was mistreated; and even Jesus cried it out on the cross. It is a general rule of thumb that the men and women God has used through the ages have suffered much and understood very well the times and seasons of the outcry, "Why?" It is a one-word question that weaves its dark strands into the fabric of all our lives.

The wise teacher, out of his life's experiences and his encounter with God, reminds us of some of his best wisdom. With the endearing term "my son," he gently urges his young student, "Do not" even begin to "despise the Lord's discipline" (3:11a). (See discussion on 1:2 for the meaning of discipline.) The teacher also adds, "Do not" even begin to "resent his rebuke" (3:11b).

Sometimes the discipline of God may be a tender word. At other times the correction may be painful mental, or physical, misfortune. The discipline and correction are intended to teach the wise disciple some valuable lessons necessary for life. Therefore, he should receive this instruction with a submissive spirit and not reject it with a spirit of resentment or rebelliousness.

Even believers sometimes find it hard to reconcile a God of goodness and love with one who permits suffering in people's lives. But that is just the point: we are dealing with a God of tender mercies who is also just and knows exactly what He is doing. He never makes mistakes. In fact, the wise teacher explains that the correction of the believer comes from the Lord because He wishes to see some desirable potential developed in us: "The Lord disciplines those he loves" (3:12a). God's care may be likened to the delight and concern our earthly fathers had for us: exactly because we were the object of their love and pride, most of us received some painful discipline. A heavenly Father can do no less, applying and permitting just the right amount and kind of correction for our eternal good and for His glory.

The problem of suffering and pain is never easily settled and, in some instances, never fully resolved. We have to regretfully recognize that some painful discipline comes as a result of laxity in believers' lives. Other trying experiences come for no reason at all except that God may be glorified in the sufferer's life, as with Job and with the blind man described in John 9. Through many different trying situations God may be able to reach others through us with the good news of salvation.

In fact, the writer to the Hebrews points out that, if there is no correction and discipline, there may be reason to suspect whether a person has a genuine relationship with God (Hebrews 12:5-6). David, the man after God's own heart, once declared in a wisdom psalm,

> It was good for me to be afflicted,
> so that I might learn your decrees.
> (Psalm 119:71)

WISDOM: MORE THAN . . . (3:13-18)

For what purpose or goal do men spend their energies and strength? Everyone ticks off his answers in rapid order: money, houses, lands, goods, power—and the more people have the more they want. Modern life becomes a never-ending, vicious cycle in the search for more and more, and the maddening pursuit brings no ultimate satisfaction.

The wise man, having learned something of life's goals, exclaims, "Blessed is the man [or, O the happinesses of the man] who finds wisdom, the man who gains understanding [or, makes a habit of gaining discrimination in judgment]" (3:13). Using wise discrimination in making right choices is the basis for all happiness. Proverbs emphasizes again that biblical wisdom is not mere intellectualism; rather, it consists of the total context of moral and spiritual knowledge based on the Word of God. Jesus emphasized the same truth, but in a little different manner, when He said, "Seek first his kingdom and his righteousness" (Matthew 6:33). Such a statement includes the wisdom of the Word that leads us to God and then on to godly living.

The wise teacher sharply contrasts the happiness of biblical wisdom with the coin of this world. The sons of men put a high price on silver and gold (3:14). People have died for these precious metals, and nations have sacrificed their honor over them. Rubies (red corals) are also considered precious (3:15*a*), but the advantage of having these costly possessions is a poor contrast to wisdom. What a person may desire of such costly items will never come close to what God can offer (3:15*b*).

What is the conclusion after assessing biblical wisdom and the most expensive objects men can have in this world? Simply this: wisdom is of the greatest value. It is *"more profitable* than silver and yields *better returns* than gold" (3:14) and is *"more precious* than rubies" (3:15*a*). Nothing in this world can compare. But, tragically, we have an upside-down world where people lay down their money and even their very lives for precious gems and gold but have little interest in God or His wisdom.

Where can a person find the formula for a meaningful and complete life? Note what the wise teacher tells his disciples in 3:16-18:

> Generally, "long life" (3:16*a*)
>
> Genuine "riches and honor" (3:16*b*)
>
> "Pleasant ways" on the road of life (3:17*a*),
>   where a person finds "peace" and is free from
>   inner worries (3:17*b*)
>
> "Paths of peace," where a godly person lives in
>   harmony with his neighbors (3:17*b*)
>
> The "tree of life" (3:18*a*)

Does this mean that a believer is to reject the wealth of this world? Not necessarily. The lesson of wisdom for the disciple is to have a right attitude toward money. If the Lord does bless a believer financially, he or she should realize that each one's wealth belongs to the Lord and is to be used for His purposes. Proper stewardship means that the title deed to one's finances and all other material goods must be placed in the Lord's hands. The believer is the trustee who has to make wise use of the Lord's monies and properties. One day he will have to give an account of how he handled his responsibilities.[2]

CONFIDENT LIVING (3:19-26)

Many offer all kinds of advice on how to live with the greatest of confidence. One author claims to have the formula for peace. A certain religion claims that it can be the guide for a life free from worry. A television speaker says that he has the solution for the problems of life. The offices of psychologists and psychiatrists are crowded by people filled with anxieties, guilt, and even deeper emotional problems. Advice is never ending. Wisdom is right when she says, "There is a way that *seems* right to a man" (14:12a). But wisdom offers five kinds of advice to the wise disciple for living with utmost confidence.

LIFE FOR MAN'S INNER BEING (3:19-22)

Where does a person find answers for life? Wisdom claims she has the answer and makes her plea to be heard. But on what basis can wisdom back her claims? She appeals to her involvement in creation and in her providential care (a discussion developed further in 8:22-31).

The "earth's foundations" were laid "by wisdom" (3:19a), who is the sum total of all intelligence grounded in God Himself. "Understanding," or discriminating judg-

2. For an extensive treatment of New Testament teaching on our stewardship of material possessions, see Gene A. Getz, *A Biblical Theology of Material Possessions* (Chicago: Moody, 1990).

ment, "set the heavens in place" (3:19b). "The deeps were divided" (3:20a), referring to God's direct involvement when He "made the expanse and separated the water under the expanse from the water above it" (Genesis 1:7), thereby allowing the earth to emerge. In God's providence He also arranged for "the clouds" to "let drop the dew" (3:20b) to provide just the right amount of moisture for growing plant life.

The teacher's endearing term "my son" is a reminder that in view of wisdom's part in the creation (vv. 19-20), the believer must "preserve sound judgment and discernment" (3:21a). Literally, the command to the believer is, do not even begin to "let them [wisdom, understanding, providence] out of [depart from] your sight" (3:21b). The wise disciple always keeps his eyes on wisdom and all her qualities; only then can he have a healthy soul. When these choices are made, the world will see the beauty of that "life" as an "ornament to grace [the] neck" (1:9; 3:22).

THE CONFIDENCE OF LIVING SECURELY (3:23)

With wisdom and her qualities provided by God, the disciple has every possibility of a life free from anxiety: "you will go on your way in safety and your foot will not stumble." Note a similar promise in Psalm 91:11-12: "he will command his angels . . . to guard you in all your ways . . . so that you will not strike your foot against a stone." The wise believer will have constant protection.

THE ASSURANCE OF REFRESHING SLEEP (3:24)

The fears and anxieties of life will not keep the wise disciple awake and in torment. Instead, he will be able to "lie down" and "not be afraid"; his or her "sleep will be sweet." This is good news to many today who, filled with fears and pressed down with nerve-wracking problems, are trying to relax and sleep by taking various tranquilizers.

NO UNEXPECTED FEAR (3:25)

The believer has a sure promise that he need not fear the unexpected, even if he faces dire circumstances. God promises complete protection from "sudden disaster or of the ruin that overtakes the wicked." If harm *is* permitted in the life of the child of God, He has allowed it for a purpose and has full knowledge of every circumstance. Note how Peter slept soundly and was not afraid, even though he faced a trial before Herod the following morning and certain execution after the hearing (Acts 12:6).

THE SURE SOURCE OF CONFIDENT LIVING (3:26)

"The Lord will be [is in the habit of being] your confidence [lit., at your side]" (3:26a). This great promise of comfort should encourage every believer. There is no reason to fear, be anxious, or fret over any event of everyday life. The wise disciple can have complete confidence because the Lord will protect him at all times and keep his "foot from being snared" (3:26b). The means for confident living is encouraged by the endearing exhortation by the wise teacher, and confident living is an assurance for every wise believer.

Practicing Some Distinctive Negatives (3:27-31)

Today's generation accentuates the positive. Preaching must be positive. We are to live positively. But the book of Proverbs includes some distinctive negatives for wise living. No apology is made for saying, "Do not." Just as degenerating buildings in run-down areas need to be blasted away and the rubble cleared before the new "high rises" go up, so the "old" needs to be removed from our lives before God can create the structure He wants in us. In no way do we suggest that an unbeliever has to reform himself before he can be a part of the family of God. We come to the Lord as we are, and He justifies us. However, in our moral and spiritual maturing, we have important decisions to make, and some of them include the negatives. The "do nots" are given by wisdom so as to allow no room for unwise decisions to even gain a toehold in our lives. The emphasis is on an immediate prohibition: "Do not even begin to. . . ."

We are told *not* even to begin to "withhold good from those who deserve it [lit., its owners]" (3:27*a*). Right now, while able to do so, we have an obligation to husbands, wives, fellow men, employers, rulers, and others. Whatever we have—money, talents, training—are not to be used selfishly. It is the height of injustice to withhold money from whom it is due or not to provide for the needy and poor "when it is in your power to act" (3:27*b*). We share with those who are in need and who can benefit by it (see Leviticus 19:13).

We are *not* even to begin to procrastinate in helping others when able to do so ("when you now have it with you"; 3:28*c*). The implication is to give quickly so as not to cause further embarrassment to the one in need by saying, for instance, "Come back later; I'll give it tomorrow" (3:28*b*). In fact, to delay is not only inconsiderate but downright unjust. Neither should employers, especially believers, withhold wages from their employees. Wisdom calls this stealing, and it is evil in God's sight (Deuteronomy 24:14-15).

We are to live peacefully and be known as peacemakers. Our task as wise believers is to quench "fires of hatred and jealousy." (See the discission of friendship in chapter 10.) We are told *not* even to begin to "envy a violent man" or "choose any of his ways" (3:31). The wise disciple must never acquire wealth by illegal means (see again 1:11-19). Illegal riches, and the power they command, are not to be the source of public delight or even of secret desire.

Such distinctive injunctions recognize the rights of others. These "no's" also teach us a character development that will produce distinctive people.

GOD'S SECRET (3:32)

We are told that the Lord has an intimate relationship with believers because He "takes the upright into his confidence" (3:32*b*). A similar thought is expressed in Psalm 25:14: "The Lord confides in those who fear him." Job also said, "When I was in my prime, . . . God's intimate friendship blessed my house" (29:4).

Confide has a two-fold basic meaning: council and counsel. The picture is that of friends sharing intimately with one another. Because Jeremiah, for example, stood in the council of God, he was able to proclaim God's words to His people (Jeremiah 23:18, 22). Therefore, wisdom says to wise disciples who walk uprightly that they have the distinct and high privilege of sitting in consultation with God.

To those who fear the Lord, wisdom promises that they have the Lord's counsel and are thereby established to stand firm in the midst of life's insecurities. Job lamented greatly during the time of his illness; but he only did so during his emotional "lows," when everything seemingly had closed in on him. His so-called friends were acting as his enemies, and when he tried to talk to the Lord, he felt as though he were talking to a wall. And yet precisely during the midst of his supreme trial God was closest to him. Even while Job's own soul was Satan's battleground, God's hand was establishing him. What a tremendous distinctive the child of God possesses. He has the ear of God at any time, and God can whisper His directives to him while on life's pathway.

In the antithetic parallel, "the violent man" appears to be successful and seems to reach his worldly aims and ambitions (3:31). But he is not, in reality, favored by God. The wicked are described as "perverse" or morally twisted (see 2:15), and their deeds are detested by God (3:32*a*). Can He hate? Certainly. The God who is holy, righteous, and just must detest what is inconsistent with His character.

Those who have acquired a godly reverence and awe are the ones who have God's intimate, confidential counsel. Someone once said that "they shall be of His cabinet council who choose rather to lie in the dust than to rise by evil arts and wicked principles." There is no morbid delight in debasing one's self; rather, humility before God is a grace that reveals His counsel and causes the wise disciple to stand established. They are welcomed into the fellowship of the established ones who have God's counsels and secrets.

The Curse of the Lord (3:32-35)

Like harsh, jangling tones are the proclamations: "the Lord detests a perverse [or, crooked] man" (3:32*a*); and "the Lord's curse is on the house of the wicked" (3:33*a*). Many think of God as a kindly old grandfather who loves all little children and has a kindly pat on the head for everyone. To think of a God full of "detesting" (or scorn) and who curses people seems, to some folk, like a throwback to the early days of man's evolutionary development, when he took refuge in gods who helped him face the fearful unknown.

We have already noted that God can hate. He is holy and righteous and, therefore, created a universe based on an absolute standard of morality, which clearly directs how to talk and where to walk. Those who proceed along this "turnpike" of life have a well-defined order of life, but God can exhibit negative emotions when this standard is flouted.

Many today do not want an absolute standard for their lives. They speak of morals as relative. Everyone, they believe, should do what is right in his or her own eyes as long as it seems right and does not "hurt" anyone else. The way some want to live is by kicking over the fences along the highway of life, but this will leave no clearly defined road, and confusion will reign. Such uncertainty leads to lawlessness, immorality, and a twisted sense of the worth and dignity of life itself.

The God who is love is also orderly. Although He may permit disorder to exist for a time, sooner or later He will step into this world's course of affairs. Because of His moral standards, He must judge (condemn) those who continue to flout His absolute guidelines. For example, prolife adherents seek to uphold the moral absolute of the sanctity of human life. Therefore, abortion is out of the question because it is a violation against life. The pro-choice group sees no reason why the life of the fetus cannot be terminated. In so deciding, they set themselves against one of God's basic moral standards. Eventually, should the majority of a nation adopt such a position, God will have no other recourse than to judge that deplorable decision.

God's curses are "on the house of the wicked" (3:33*a*) who scorn and mock God and His standards. He, too, "mocks proud mockers" (3:34*a*), but takes no pleasure when His judgment is at the expense of sinners. The fact that He has to scorn and mock evil men, men made in His image, only breaks His heart (Hosea 11:8). But He does laugh derisively at those who insist on standards that can only lead to chaos and ruin (Psalm 2:1-4).

The wise disciple who seeks to do His will enjoys intimate fellowship with God and has specific guaranteed promises. A series of antithetic parallel statements promise the believer (1) blessing upon his "house" (3:33*b*), (2) the provision of "grace to the humble" (3:34*b*) when he has to suffer at times for the glory of God, and (3) an inheritance of "honor" (3:35*a*) accorded to him by the very Lord of the universe. The conclusion of the matter is that we are to flee God's curse and find the Lord's blessings.

My son, pay attention to what I say;
listen closely to my words.

Proverbs 4:20

4

THE FATHER AND THE TEACHER (4:1-27)

We have already seen how important wisdom is to the believer and that it is more precious than anything else in this world, whether money, fame, or position. The study of the words of wisdom in Proverbs can help us to *appropriate* God's purposes for our spiritual benefit. If the disciples in God's school will be wise to *live* the will of God, they will be encouraged in their pursuit of godliness, vital faith, and confidence.

The focus of Proverbs 4 is wisdom and the family. Here the wisdom of God becomes critical. Who is going to teach in our families? To whom has God entrusted the awesome task of training children? Israel had its God-appointed office of the sage, whose function was to teach. But did this mean there was no role for the father to also teach and train his own children? Such teaching is critical, especially when we realize that a child's character is largely shaped and formed by the time he or she is three years of age. What does God expect in a home, even before a child is placed in a formal academic situation?

In this lesson we note how God holds the father and mother responsible to cultivate a spiritual atmosphere in the home so that a child can come to know the Lord and learn the first principles of wisdom for godly living. Though unbelievers may certainly impart basic morals to their children, only parents who have a born-again experience with the Lord can adequately teach their children sound reasons to believe and do God's will.

THE FATHER IS THE TEACHER (4:1-4)

These verses describe what is a lost art in our generation. Wisdom provides the picture of a devout home where the father sits in the midst of his children and teaches them the ways of God. This portrait contrasts with the scene of varied interests in the average home today, where regular Bible reading is hardly practiced, and prayer around the family altar is unknown.

The opening verses in this chapter do not merely depict a teacher assuming the character of a father addressing his disciples in endearing language. If we take seriously that Solomon wrote these passages, and if words are taken at their face value, then three generations are described here: "When I was a boy in my father's house, still tender, and an only child of my mother . . ." (4:3). Solomon was actually reflecting on his parents, David and Bathsheba. In a unique sense he was especially chosen by God to be king over Israel: "David said to the whole assembly, 'My son Solomon, the one whom God has chosen . . . '" (1 Chronicles 29:1); and "They named him Solomon . . . and because the Lord loved him, he sent word through Nathan the prophet to name him Jedidiah [or, loved by the Lord]" (2 Samuel 12:24-25). But Solomon also said to *his* children, "Listen, my sons, to a father's instruction [or, disciplinary instruction]" (4:1a); he described for us how he yearned for the well-being of his own children.

David, as a godly father, laid the foundation in Solomon's life. By no means, however, was Israel's sweet singer perfect. At times, by bitter experience, he learned many lessons in God's school of wisdom. But he did teach Solomon, and in words just short of a positive command, the future king was told by his father to "lay hold of my words with all your heart; keep my commands and you will live" (4:4). Is it any wonder then that Solomon was right to choose wisdom when confronted by God at the beginning of his reign?

Solomon followed in David's steps at this point of his spiritual experience, and he urged his children to "pay attention and gain understanding" (4:1b) and "not forsake my teaching [or, law]" (4:2b). Even though he later failed in so many ways, he at least knew his responsibilities.

Here is the rightful place of the father in his relationship to his children. Today he has almost forsaken his God-given task. Many a mother has performed nobly, but how much better to have a godly father as leader in the home. Both parents can then rear their sons and daughters to live for the Lord. Godly offspring are no accident; godly fathers must discipline and guide their sons and daughters as "a heritage from the Lord" (Psalm 127:3).

THE FATHER TEACHES THE LOVE THAT COUNTS (4:5-9)

Today, the word *love* is tossed around to describe a variety of activities and attitudes:

> The four time divorced actress now "loves" her fifth fiancé.
> The mother "loves" her son, who is making his mark in the world.
> The young man "loves" to have a good time.
> The ten-year-old girl "loves" chocolate sodas.

These "loves" contrast so superficially with God's love: "For God so loved the world that he gave his one and only son. . ." (John 3:16).

The Lord reminds the earthly father that he has to teach the kind of love that matters most in this life. Wisdom is presented as a woman to be courted. The highest and best in life will be provided by this most gracious lady. She will meet all the needs and provide all the necessary guidance that anyone could ever want: "She will protect you; love her, and she will watch over you" (4:6a-b).

The children are commanded to love wisdom; that is, they are to put their whole being into this endeavor ("embrace her"; 4:8*b*). They are further commanded to "trade" everything they possess to obtain a "shoe leather" wisdom: "Get wisdom. Though it cost all you have, get understanding [or, discriminatory judgment]" (4:7*b-c*). The progression of the word arrangement is important: first, get wisdom; then, get understanding, or discernment. The initial emphasis is never on the intellect but, instead, on the kind of wisdom that leads to moral living and action.

Still another command reminds the father to teach his children to have a high regard for wisdom: "esteem her" (4:8*a*). Young ones are told not to even begin to "forsake wisdom" (4:6*a*), because they will never have a better life's companion than godly wisdom. In return, she will "honor" (4:8*b*) her devoted ones. She will help in every good decision in life to ultimately "set a garland of grace on" the head of the believer and present him "with a crown of splendor" (4:9).

All of these fatherly lessons represent a distinct clash with worldly wisdom and pursuits that do not necessarily provide the right moral guidance. Perhaps an excellent illustration of love is that which Jacob had for Rachel. In spite of all the restrictions he suffered at the hands of Laban, we are told that the long years of service "seemed like only a few days to him because of his love for her" (Genesis 29:20). Life may be a hard taskmaster, but as we search the Word of God and seek to conform and bend our wills to this Word, God's wisdom will make life's experiences bearable. The fatherly love that counts can lift us from the lowest levels to the highest heights in every experience of life.

THE FATHER TEACHES THE WAY OF WISDOM (4:10-13, 18)

The whale under pursuit turned and rammed the whaling ship with such impact that it began to sink rapidly. The life boats were loaded and lowered, and managed to pull away to safety. No sooner were all the men at a safe distance than two of them jumped into the water and swam back to the ship about to go down. Only with great difficulty and at great risk did they salvage what was worth more than their mortal lives in that predicament: *the compass.* Whatever else was lost, they needed the compass, for *it was their life* to guide the way through the trackless sea.

The father continues in his effort to teach his children how to be guided by wisdom's compass. The right kind of life, he admonishes, has a path that leads to a specific destination. A father must continually guide his children "in the way of wisdom"; they are to also "listen" and "accept" what he says so that the years of their lives "will be many" (4:10-11a). Wisdom leads "along the straight paths" (4:11b), which steadily approaches its objectives. There are no by-passes leading into rutted paths, swamps, chuck holes, or dead-ends. This is a *broad* turnpike where, regardless of whether one "walks" or "runs," the going should never be in distress or anxiety; in those life situations where fast decisions and actions are necessary, wisdom will not let her followers be "hampered" in any way or allow them to "stumble" (4:12; Isaiah 40:31). These lessons prepare the child for life's storms where, despite physical pain or emotional pressure, the mature person need not be "anxious" (Philippians 4:6-7).

The father-teacher advises his children of the source of strength on the way of life. His children are to "hold on to" disciplinary "instruction" (which, in this case, is parental counsel) and not even begin to "let go" of its benefits (4:13; 1:13). So important is this kind of instruction that the young person is advised to "guard it well, for it is your life" (4:13b). The reader should take note, however, that the father is the one who has to impart wisdom and instruction—which is life itself—to his children.

There may seem to be a contrast between this and what Jesus described in Matthew 7:13, but no contradiction is intended. The father stresses the *experience of result,* in which the disciple finds that the way of wisdom brings no heartaches, distress, or discouragements that cannot be resolved. Jesus emphasizes the difficulty of *experience in process* that will cost the disciple all he has to walk in the way of righteousness. Both facets of the truth are necessary, and the father-teacher agrees with these sentiments (4:7b).

The way of wisdom has the glory of God as its ultimate goal (4:18). What an objective to cultivate in your children early in their lives. The righteous walk on a path that "is like the first gleam of dawn, shining ever brighter till the full light of day," when they will finally be in the presence of God in all His glory.

THE FATHER DESCRIBES THE WAY
OF WICKEDNESS (4:14-17, 19)

The way of wickedness is presented in sharp contrast to the way of wisdom. The father must take the responsibility to teach his children about the habits and ways of evil men. The father's own *descriptive knowledge* based on wisdom derived from God's revelation is sufficient for moral guidance as to what is sin. He does not have to actually partake of *knowledge* gained by *experience* to know something of the effects of sin.

We must be realistic with our children and teach them that we live in a world of sin. Too many parents want to hide from their offspring all the unpleasant areas of life. But we have to point out the situations that reflect the effects of fallen nature and yet also focus on how the power of Christ changes lives so that the potential for sin can be minimized. Unless we share with our children both the way of wisdom *and* the way of wickedness, we will end up providing a lop-sided view of life. Wisdom teaches that we must detest sin, but at the same time we need to have compassion for the sinner.

The overpowering strength and rapid sequence of the verbs of this passage stress the awful road of wickedness. The commands are aimed with accurate intent: "Do not" even begin to "set foot on the path of the wicked"; do not even begin to "walk [or, be guided to find happiness] in the way of evil men" (4:14). Avoid it; "do not" even begin to "travel on it" (or, "pass by the way of wickedness"); "turn from it [the road of destruction] and go on your way" (4:15). These warnings could not be couched in stronger language.

The father's *descriptive knowledge* of sin continues. The kind of men who travel the path of wickedness are restless: "they cannot sleep till they do evil" (4:16*a*). Their lives are overcome by wicked desires: "they are robbed of slumber till they make someone fall [or, stumble]" (4:16*b*) to accomplish their lawless desires and deeds. Contrast this life-style with the righteous who can enjoy sweet sleep when they lie down (3:24).

We are created to worship, but if godly wisdom is not in control, then self becomes the tyrant in one way or another, leading to thievery, robbery, adultery, and murder. In fact, the symbol of "food" or "bread," normally used to picture the time of joy with our families at dinner time, becomes a perversion for evil men to satisfy the soul when "they eat the bread of wickedness and drink the wine of violence" (4:17).

The goal of the wicked is a terrifying one. Obedient disciples find the Lord, begin to walk in His light in the way of wisdom, and finally stand in His glory. By contrast the evil reject wisdom and her way. "The way of the wicked" becomes increasingly enveloped in "deep darkness" (4:19*a*), and eventually the path is covered with a thick blackness, such as the Egyptians experienced (Exodus 10:22). Evil people will "not know what makes them stumble" (4:19*b*), but suddenly they will topple over, separated from God forever because the darkness of their way blinds them to their coming misfortune. When people do not heed wisdom, they will end up in eternity, forever unhappy and unfulfilled.

WE SHOULD CHECK OUR MOTIVES (4:20-23)

On many occasions it becomes necessary to check out our motives for the decisions we make and activities in which we are engaged. Those around us see only an outside profile, but God sees the heart and probes the motives on the inside, where an altogether different picture prevails.

After being reminded to "pay attention" and "listen closely" to the words of wisdom (4:20), the child-disciple is to told to "keep" these precepts "within [his] heart" (4:21*b*). Instructions are further given to "guard [the] heart" because it is more important than anything else (4:23*a*): from it is the "wellspring [or, out-going] of life" (4:23*b*). Just as the heart was recognized as the central organ pumping the life's blood throughout the body, so, as a metaphor, the heart came to stand for the inner being of a person, which morally conditions all his activities.

This concern to guard the heart is important because it is easily the most precious possession committed to a man's trust; he is, therefore, held responsible for it. If the heart is pure, the life will be pure. If the heart is corrupt, the life is corrupt. In fact, the heart is compared to a fountain: from this seat of affections and center of moral consciousness flow the currents of life to the world of humanity around us.

The "greater than Solomon," Jesus Christ, built one of His most important messages on this concept. All the evil thoughts, murders, adulteries, and evil actions of men come from within the heart. A man is not made "unclean" by the food he eats or by what clothing he wears. He becomes unclean because the inner being is not right (Matthew 15:19-20), and corruption proceeds from within to the outside.

Godly wisdom leads the disciple to a change in his inner being. When he pays attention to the teacher's sayings and inclines his heart, yielding to God's wisdom (based on a revelation), the result will be a supernatural life-style. The test of motives will either reveal the presence of a supernatural life or an inward profile that is only a sham. "Testing our motives" is tantamount to a heart check.

A Medical Examination of Righteousness (4:24-27)

Which of us, at one time or another, has not been subjected to a doctor's examination? The doctor asks us to stick out our tongues. He looks into our eyes, sticks his special instrument into our ears, and listens to our hearts. He pokes at our stomachs, taps our knees for the right reflexes, and examines our feet. In the same way, wisdom examines the disciple to determine the state of his moral and spiritual health.

In this part of the text, the father, in his role as the teacher of wisdom, takes on the task of being a spiritual and moral doctor. The wisdom he teaches examines the mouth. Is it "perverse," or crooked (4:24a)? Does the mouth falsify truth and speak evil? If so, the disciple must "put away perversity from [his] mouth" before evil consequences result.

How is the state of the lips? Do they turn aside from righteousness to speak evil? The advice is to "keep corrupt talk far from your lips" (4:24b). As we shall see later (chapter 11), God has a scathing medical prognosis for those who wrongly use the mouth and tongue. A vain, polluted, biting, or untruthful tongue can only bring disrepute to the family of God.

What is the condition of the eyes? Do they stare without purpose, glance to the right or to the left, or look curiously in an immoral manner? Wicked and evil people have that shifty and furtive look (6:13), but the prescription by wisdom is that the "eyes look straight ahead" and "fix" their "gaze [or, eyelids] directly" ahead (4:25) in the delight of beholding what is right. The eyelids are a metaphor for "gazing," and the test concerns whether a person's gaze is fixed upon an aim or goal that leads to the highest spiritual achievements.

The Lord Jesus described this further when He said that the lamp of the body depends on the eye. If the "eyes are good," that is, fixed on spiritual goals, then the "whole body will be full of light" (Matthew 6:22). Spiritual crosseye needs to be corrected.

The feet are also examined. Are they spiritually and morally lame, club- or flat-footed, making it difficult to walk in the right way? Wisdom prescribes that feet "make level paths" (4:26a) or "consider carefully" where they intend to walk: "Take only ways that are firm. Do not even begin to swerve to the right or left; keep your foot from evil" (4:26b-27). The believer must avoid evil deviations. A periodic moral and spiritual medical examination is essential.

5

A PLEA FOR CHASTITY
(5:1-35; 6:20-35; 7:1-27)

After considering the importance of parents in the God-given role of the father as teacher in the home, wisdom now turns to one specific and prominent area: sexual morality and purity. This theme was introduced in the discussion of 2:16-19, but this subject occurs repeatedly in Proverbs because the father was expected to devote attention to it in training his children. In a more formal way, the sage also elaborated on the necessity for sexual purity.

Not only was adultery a sin against God because it violated the seventh commandment; there was also a definite connection between adultery and idolatry in the pagan religions contemporary with ancient Israel. Part of the worship systems of the Canaanites and other Middle Eastern countries included the satisfaction of sensual desires. At temple shrines priests and priestesses engaged in sexual immorality. For this reason, spiritual idolatry led many times to physical adultery. But even if sexual impurity has no ties to the practice of pagan religions, it is still an offense against God and His moral standards.

So as to prepare young people to respect the God-ordained pattern for marriage, the father and sage are to encourage their charges to cultivate wholesome attitudes toward one another and with the opposite sex. Young people are to learn that each human being is a person created in the image of God and that, in the marriage relationship, the husband and wife should have the highest regard for each other. The breakdown of the marriage relationship because of adultery not only demeans one's marital partner, it also degrades God, who has made each of us in His image.

LOOSE MORALS HAVE A PRICE TAG (5:1-14)

Today's generation may appear pure in its own eyes, but according to Proverb's description of moral anarchy, most people are not "cleansed of their filth" (30:12). Many today rationalize their immoral conduct in appealing words: "the New Morality," "liberated," "free," and "gay." They resent any labeling of their life-style as "loose morals" and insist that their conduct is not really wrong at all. But built into the moral fiber of the universe is a penalty to be paid when God's moral standards are tossed aside.

The teacher repeats his earnest caution in the words of wisdom because he is particularly concerned for the welfare of the young. He describes the temptations of sin: "lips" that "drip honey" and deceive with speech that is "smoother than oil" (5:3). This descriptive knowledge does not deny the possibility of these pleasures, but the cost of illicit sex puts a crushing mortgage on the soul and eventually leads to eternal separation from God.

Wisdom points out the high price tag for immorality. An illicit life robs a person of his "best strength" and "years" (5:9). A young man loses his vitality and youthful bearing when he gives the prime years of his life and happiness to the immoral woman and her accomplices. But the cost increases: the man who indulges in this kind of life leaves his "wealth" and the fruit of his "toil" in the houses of "strangers" (5:10). What a waste. We must learn that God's morals can never be thrust aside without paying the price.

By no means does wisdom pin all the blame on the man. The immoral woman has little to show for the years of her illicit "take." In the end, she also pays, and "her feet go down to death; her steps lead straight to the grave [literally, *sheol*]" (5:5), to the place where the dead go. Another part of the price of immorality is physical disease: "At the end of your life you will groan, when your flesh and body are spent" (5:11). A life of immorality for both men and women subjects them to any one of several social diseases that can cripple, maim, and even rob of sanity. Of special concern today is AIDS, which is frequently not only the bitter fruit of homosexuality but also of illicit heterosexual relations.

Such a life for self brings with it inner remorse, an accusing conscience, and the mental torture of wasted years when listening to godly wisdom might have spared such havoc: "How I have hated discipline! How my heart spurned correction! I would not obey my teachers or listen to my instructors" (5:12-13).

The teacher has to mention the ultimate cost of this ruin. Such offenders were stoned to death (Deuteronomy 22:22). So as to underscore how serious is the crime of immorality, the law had no sacrifice to prescribe for such folly in Israel. Is this too high a price for sin? No. The very moral and social fabric of Israel had to be preserved. For their own welfare, the people had to realize how grave was this offense and understand the importance of obeying God's moral absolutes.

A note of pathos is heard as one surveys the wreckage of wasted years: "I have come to the brink of utter ruin in the midst of the whole assembly" (5:14). The teacher, therefore, warns the young to stay away from the temptation of loose living because the price tag of immorality is too high for the moral pocketbook. Why go down to death (5:5-6a)?

FAMILY FIDELITY SATISFIES BEST (5:15-23)

Wisdom now takes a welcomed turn from the high cost of loose morals to the legitimate and best pleasures of a recognized marriage. Natural desires and basic urges are God-given for every man and woman to enjoy, and these can be satisfied while the heart and the conscience are kept pure. The teacher wants his disciples to know that family faithfulness is best. Using one of the few allegories found in the book of Proverbs, the teacher describes the exhilaration of cold water in an otherwise dry and hot climate. How refreshing cool water feels to a person with parched tongue and lips, desperately craving relief from his thirst. The teacher now draws the parallel: "May your fountain be blessed, and may you rejoice in the wife of your youth" (5:18). By means of poetic parallelism (see Introduction), he compares this fountain of cool water to the lovely charms of the wife and first love, which is supposed to satisfy all the basic urges of both husband and wife.

Furthermore, this emphasis on "your own cistern," "your own well," and "your springs" points to the satisfaction possible within the marriage frame (5:15-17). "Springs [that] overflow in the streets" (5:16a) are probably an image of the children of such a marriage. Blessing, therefore, streams forth among those in a family honored by the Lord.

The teacher's main emphasis here is to demonstrate to his young disciples that basic human sexual urges can be satisfied in an honorable way, without recourse to acts of foolishness: "Why be captivated, my son, by an adulteress? Why embrace the bosom of another man's wife?" (5:20). He is to remain faithful to the wife of his youth. Neither should a wife forget the lover of her youth and seek satisfaction with other men.

No one should object to the erotic language that also occurs often in the Song of Solomon. The culture in which God's Word was given was not prudish. When it suited wisdom best, she was quite candid with what was proper in the expression of love. Just as the teacher drew on descriptive language to picture the horrors of the high cost of immorality, he is equally descriptive to make attractive the God-given sexual delight enjoyed within marriage. The lasting, tender love of a young husband and wife as pictured by wisdom is to be our model for believers and unbelievers alike.

IMMORALITY IS STUPID (6:24-35)

The teacher of wisdom keeps hammering away at the theme of chastity. He is not satisfied merely mentioning the high price tag of sexual impurity or painting the picture of family fidelity in the most desirable of terms. Now he wants to also point out that the immoral person is a stupid fool. Do these words sound harsh? The teacher wants to be sure his disciples will not miss the message.

As the disciples mature—if they would be wise—they will keep away "from the smooth tongue of the wayward wife," will not lust after "her beauty," and not be captivated "with her eyes" (6:24b-25). But the fellow who would be stupid enough to risk poverty, not to mention his very life, to pursue such so-called love will learn that "the prostitute reduces you to a loaf of bread, and the adulteress preys upon your very life" (6:26).

Such "love-making" elicits some hard questions: Can a man make a habit of scooping "fire into his lap"? (6:27a); can a man make a habit of walking "on hot coals"? (6:28a). Of course not, for in either case, he would burn himself severely: "his clothes" will be burned, and "his feet" will be scorched (6:27b, 28b). With great yearning, but with sharp reproof, wisdom warns the inexperienced and naive that the vice of immorality has a disastrous chain of cause and effect. Any who would caress his neighbor's wife is not innocent and will suffer the consequences of his actions: "No one who touches her will go unpunished" (6:29b).

Wisdom continues this lesson by making a difficult comparison: a person can be so poor that he resorts to "stealing to satisfy his hunger when he is starving" (6:30b). When caught, he must pay sevenfold, thereby forfeiting "all the wealth of his house" (6:31), which will reduce him to poverty. The law in Israel called for different penalties for various kinds of theft: five-fold for an ox if it was then slaughtered or sold; if sheep were stolen and either slaughtered or sold, the penalty was four-fold (Exodus 22:1). However, "if the stolen animal is found alive in his possession whether ox or donkey or sheep—he must pay back double" (22:3). When a farmer knows he has a bull that has the habit of goring other animals and does not keep it penned up, then he must repay, animal for animal, what his bull had destroyed (Exodus 21:37). But nowhere does the law call for such extreme restitution as a seven-fold repayment by a poor person caught in his wrong-doing. We can only conclude that wisdom's directive for such a restitution was to emphasize how costly is thievery. However, once the thief has paid his penalty, he will not be despised.

But the stupid fellow "who commits adultery with a woman lacks judgment [literally, a heart of understanding]" (6:32a). Doesn't he know that "jealousy" will arouse her "husband's fury" when he finds out (6:34a)? The word for "husband" expresses the dimension of his strength, and the word picture conveys that this offended husband will use all his manly strength "when he takes revenge" on the offender (6:34b). The poor thief can square his debt and not be despised, but an offended husband will "show no mercy" on his culprit.

Nor will any amount of money rectify the situation. An adulterer can never pay enough "compensation" to wipe out the affront to the offended husband's honor; in fact, the husband "will refuse" any "bribe, however great it is" (6:35). The stupid fool who commits adultery is in "disgrace" and "his shame will never be wiped away" (6:33). As already mentioned, the Mosaic constitution called for both adulterer and adulteress to be put to death, since there was no sacrifice to cover this "high-handed" sin (Deuteronomy 22:22). Wisdom cries "stupid" to anyone involved in illicit love. Let the young and inexperienced have a heart of understanding.

THE TEMPTRESS ENTICES (7:5-27)

Even while the teacher was sharing his important lessons on sexual purity and morality, the stupidity of adultery, and the desirability of family fidelity, he looked out the window and observed a tragic example of what was detestable. There, before his very eyes, was the scene of a young man being enticed by an attractive temptress. What he saw and heard became the subject of a compelling lesson about the vice of immorality.

The naive and experienced lad, in need of wisdom and lacking "judgment" (lit., heart; 7:7c), was probably wandering aimlessly. The unexpected place and the timing of temptation were against him: "He was going down the street near her corner, walking along in the direction of her house at twilight, as the day was fading, as the dark of night set in" (7:8-9). The teacher carefully explains how the temptress is dressed in her most appealing clothes to attract her paramours, but inwardly she guards ("with crafty intent") how she really feels (7:10b). She wants to indulge herself, however, and she looks diligently—"now in the street, now in the squares, at every corner" (7:12)—for the right person, one she believes can satisfy her desires. But does this really meet a woman's needs? Hardly.

The teacher graphically describes her crafty plan for attracting her victim. She kisses the young man (7:13a) as if to impress him that she really cares for him. She gives him, of all the excuses, that she is really a pious woman: "I have peace offerings at home; today I have fulfilled my vows" (7:14). How could he refuse her by ignoring such expressions of love on a day of celebration? She has offered her peace offering (no doubt at some shrine of pagan worship), and after giving the portion that belonged to the priests, she had the rest of the meat in the house for a good meal (Leviticus 7:28-33; 15-17). Not only will the young man be able to enjoy the sexual relationship, but there will be plenty to eat as well.

The temptress also uses flattery—"I came out to meet you; I looked for you and have found you!" (7:15) —as if he is the very one who could make her happy. If the young man should hesitate, she knows to appeal strongly to his sensuous desires: "I have covered my bed with colored linens from Egypt. I have perfumed my bed with myrrh, aloes and cinnamon. Come, let's drink deep of love till morning; let's enjoy ourselves with love!" (7:16-18). It will be a night long to be remembered. Finally the young man is relieved of all fears when he is assured, "My husband is not at home; he has gone on a long journey. He took his purse filled with money and will not be home till full moon" (7:19-20). In fact, she speaks of her husband as "the man," a contemptuous term to create the impression that she doesn't care for him. How could she really care for her husband with her kind of life-style?

Sadly, the teacher describes this naive youth, perhaps hesitating in indecision for a while, but "all at once" in a moment of weakness his resistance melts (7:22a). Because of his tragic decision, he is "like an ox going to the slaughter" (7:22b) or "a bird darting into a snare" (7:23b). "Little knowing it will cost him his life" (7:23c), he engages in stolen love. Both, however, are considered offenders and liable to the sentence of death.

In a concluding plea, the teacher warns his charges to "pay attention" (7:24b) and not to let their hearts "turn to her ways or stray into her paths" (7:25). Young people must keep away from places of temptation and mark well how foolish are the prostitute's naive victims. Such questionable enjoyment can only lead to dissipation and other crimes, and in the end "the grave" and "the chambers of death" (7:27). The word of the temptress is the way to a trap.

THE WORD OF GOD DEFUSES TEMPTATION (6:20-24; 7:1-4)

We come to the end of this impassioned plea for sexual purity and marital faithfulness. At stake in that day was the protection of Israel's social fabric; still at stake today is the stability of social structures. The lack of sexual morality in our society is translated into broken homes, shattered adult lives, and irreversible harm to children caught in these tragedies.

The best advice is to avoid immorality by carefully considering what the wisdom of the Word of God declares and then translating the lessons into everyday habits. Temptation will ever be present, but we do have the means to overcome evil influences and find the way of escape.

Wisdom speaks in words that remind us of 1:8 (see chapter 1): "My son, keep your father's commands and do not forsake your mother's teaching" (6:20). By means of metaphor, God's "commands" are identified with "a lamp" (6:23a). These commands direct a man to do what is good and avoid evil, and, even more basic, they illumine minds and hearts to discern the moral opposites of good and evil. We are reminded here that the Word is a lamp to our feet, to direct our steps (Psalm 119:105). Furthermore, "this teaching" (lit., Torah), or divine instruction, "is light" (6:23b). Because this instruction is given by God, the individual must listen diligently to be enlightened. The reproofs of disciplinary instruction are not intended to be difficult; in fact, "the corrections of discipline are the way to life" (6:23c-d).

God's laws help us to establish good *habits*. The commands are to be kept "as the apple [or, pupil] of [the] eye" (7:2b), the body's most precious part and, perhaps, the most delicate organ.

Wisdom's words and commandments are to be bound upon the "fingers" and written upon the tablets of one's "heart" (7:3). They must have a place in a person's entire understanding. People are to be occupied with the Word of God, which establishes the work of their hands and helps them find good paths for their feet. Wisdom desires to guide in all the affairs of life; therefore, she must be regarded with honor and accorded the dignity of a "sister" (7:4a). The naive are also encouraged to diligently seek "understanding" (or, discriminatory judgment), esteeming her highly as a kinsperson (7:4b), much like the kinsman-redeemer, who lovingly did all in his power to redeem his near of kin (Ruth 2:1; 3:2; 4:1-9). Godly habits should become as much a part of us as the close-knit and highly respected female members of our families.

We are forewarned and fortified, having the means to keep us "from the immoral woman" and "from the smooth tongue of the wayward wife" (6:24). God can give us victory over every temptation. God's Word is stronger than temptation's wiles.

There are six things the Lord hates,
seven that are detestable to him: . . .
a man who stirs up dissension among brothers.

Proverbs 6:16, 19*b*

6

FOLLIES TO AVOID (6:1-19)

Wisdom has not exhausted the meaning of immorality. Besides sexual impurity, it has a much wider meaning, and wherever man goes, his sin nature can mar human relationships and break moral absolutes.

A study of the book of Proverbs gives us divine wisdom in how to relate to our families, friends, communities, and leaders. Often it is not *how much* we say to people, although that is important; it is *what* we say. The source of our wisdom is Scripture, where we find basic answers to life. Scripture provides our guideline for a godly life-style on the avenues of life. Many a person has come to faith through the combined influence of a believer's life-style and verbal witness.

In Proverbs 6 the wisdom teacher instructs the naive and inexperienced to avoid the pitfalls of the bad business deal, laziness, lying and cheating, brawling, and the fighting spirit.

THE FOLLY OF OVEREXTENDED DEBT (6:1-5)

Unlimited debt is a foolishness for which Wisdom has some severe warnings.[1] The Mosaic Covenant encouraged people to help one another, especially those who had unexpected financial difficulties. When loans were involved, no interest was to be charged (Leviticus 25:35-38). In particular, land sales were carefully regulated because the family plot of land was never to be sold. All a purchaser could buy from a needy farmer was the crop value to the next year of Jubilee, at which time the use of the land reverted back to the family who owned it (Leviticus 25:13-16).

Sometimes, when one entered into business negotiations, he might not have enough financial reserves or collateral to assure the loan. He or she would then call on someone to guarantee the loan. If the debtor could not pay back on his loan, the one who "put up security" would have to make good on it.

In many cases, because of a friend's distress or a genuine willingness to help, a young person would be prone to strike his "hands in pledge" (6:1) and formally assure a debt. But such hastiness to become collateral often reflects financial inexperience and leads to becoming "trapped by what [was] said" and "ensnared by . . . words" (6:2). Rash words and impulsive promises can be dangerous. Whoever makes the loan might be unable to repay, having unwittingly overextended himself. Both would then be brought into ruin because such business practices are foolish. Even though generosity was not to be discouraged, the promise to make good beyond a person's means was nothing less than gambling.

A person in such a predicament was commanded to do all in his power to rid himself of the debt: "free yourself since you have fallen into your neighbor's hands" (6:3). He was to "humble" himself (6:4c), and the word pictures a person who has allowed himself to be trampled

---

1. Also see Larry Burkett, *Debt-Free Living: How to Get Out of Debt (and Stay Out)* (Chicago: Moody, 1989).

on. He was to strongly press his plea with his neighbor (6:3*d*). This advice sounds much like Jesus' story of the friend who at midnight asked "persistently" for bread (Luke 11:8). Wisdom advises, therefore, "Allow no sleep [Do not even begin to allow sleep] to your eyes, no slumber to your eyelids. Free yourself, like a gazelle from the hand of the hunter, like a bird from the snare of the fowler" (6:4-5). The implication is to quickly seek freedom from obligation and not to fritter away time or delay the opportunity to be rid of such an imposing obligation.

In a day of easy credit, Wisdom's advice is not to overextend our debts beyond our means to pay. Watch what dotted line to which you sign your name.

The Folly of Laziness (6:6-11)

Wisdom now addresses herself to the foolishness of being lazy (see also chapter 11). This may not be a popular lesson, but the appeal is to be diligent in everything.

The teacher commands the lazy person to "go to the ant" and "consider its ways and be wise" (6:6). Even though the ant is such a small creature, it is an example of diligence and hard work. The illustration is two-fold: first, the ant does not *appear* to need a "commander, . . . overseer or ruler" (6:7), whereas the lazy one must be prodded. In fact, he is immobile until someone comes along and tries to stir him up, and even then it is extremely difficult to get the person to move. Second, the ant colony seems to have some sense of time. Ants store their "provisions in summer" and gather their "food at harvest" time (6:8). But the lazy person has no concept of time. To the slothful, all time is alike. He enjoys his nap time, slumber, and snoozing: "A little sleep, a little slumber, a little folding of the hands to rest" (6:10). This is the response of the lazy man when he ought to be preparing for winter. The teacher wants his charges to learn to be as diligent as the ants.

Wisdom also invites her listeners to consider the bitter lesson of poverty. If the young man will not listen, and avoid the foolishness of being lazy, he will wake up from his nap one day to find that "poverty [has] come on [him] like a bandit and scarcity like an armed man" (6:11). The text first pictures a bandit who pounces unexpectedly on the traveler and leaves him penniless. The second image is that of the armed man (or a man of the shield) who, much like invading soldiers, will plunder and strip bare a town. So the idler becomes impoverished.

The wise person will learn while there is time. After all, a person is lazy because he or she conditions life with too many excuses and postponements. The pattern becomes so easy—procrastination, relaxation, sleeping—and soon every area of life is affected. Decision-making capacities become stifled, and in the end the lazy person becomes the loser. Laziness is foolishness. *Sleepy sluggards become destiny's derelicts.*

The Folly of Mischief (6:12-15)

Undue mischief is foolishness. This does not mean that believers must avoid joy in life. But the misguided pleasure seeker is the person who causes trouble by quiet subtleties until a full-scale fight erupts.

Wisdom *describes* the *inner motives* and *priorities* of the mischiefmaker as that of a scoundrel and sharply denounces him as, literally, "a man of Belial" (6:12a). The word *Belial* means "of no profit" and "good for nothing," but the word always describes the person who has an evil character: "Eli's sons were wicked men," "sons of Belial" (1 Samuel 2:12), and when Jezebel wanted to do away with Naboth, she called for "two scoundrels," or literally, "two men, sons of Belial," to testify that they had heard Naboth curse God and the king (1 Kings 21:10).

But the "scoundrel" is also a "villain," literally, "a man of iniquity" (6:12a). The latter term is well chosen because he lacks integrity, departing from doing what is right. He is further described as plotting "evil with deceit [or, perversity] in his heart" (6:14). The heart, which is perverse, continually turns things upside down (see discussion at 2:14). To such a person, good is wrong and evil right. He has a twisted personality.

This type of person *acts outwardly* in a predictable manner. What is on the inside will soon become apparent on the outside. He "goes about with a corrupt mouth" (6:12*b*), and as he makes the rounds of his favorite haunts, he plants the seed of his mischievous slander among friends and neighbors. He has a malicious way of winking "with his eye" to insinuate that the person of whom he speaks is guilty of evil intentions or implicated of wrong doing. The scoundrel also "signals with his feet," probably in some prearranged signal to his cronies to tag some innocent victim; he "motions with his fingers" (6:13) as he accuses someone unjustly, and the gang closes in on the helpless individual falsely charged. Without speaking a word, the mischievous person, this man of iniquity, continually "plots evil with deceit in his heart" and "always stirs [or, is in the habit of stirring] up dissension" (6:15) between people.

It seems as if this man of mischief will never stop, but God's hour will strike for him. The *end* for this person is "disaster," which "will overtake him in an instant; he will suddenly be destroyed—without remedy [or, healing]" (6:14). Sudden death can be regarded as a divine judgment. Even the patience of God wears thin when a person continually persists in a life of mischief.

THE HATRED OF GOD (6:16)

One of the most jolting of all realizations is that, while God is a God of love, He can hate in a very real way. Certain attitudes and activities are detested by God.

The figures of "six" and "seven" (6:16) do not suggest that this list exhausts everything God hates. Rather, it seems to be a figure of speech to help one remember some of these sins of shame and abhorrence. The enumeration of numbers appears elsewhere in the Old Testament with the same apparent purpose as a memory device: "From six calamities he will rescue you; in seven no harm will befall you" (Job 5:19); "Give portions to seven, yes to eight" (Ecclesiastes 11:2); "seven shepherds, even eight leaders of men" (Micah 5:5*d-e*).

Anger is another term that sometimes depicts God's feelings. The word picture is that of a red nose, which is an apt illustration of what happens when anger is aroused; the nose and face become red with violent emotion. God's responses fit this posture when His anger is directed against sin.

A number of passages describe such a violent emotion when God exhibits complete righteous indignation. When Korah and "certain Reubenites" rebelled against Moses, questioning his authority, wrath came "out from the Lord," and a plague began to consume all who took their stand against God and His anointed leaders (Numbers 16:1, 46). God is a "jealous God" (Exodus 20:5), and those who choose to be His enemies will one day experience His consuming fire, swallowed up by His wrath (Psalm 21:9).

Our sovereign God will in many instances select certain nations and permit them to commit atrocities against His people. In the past, He has used nations as an instrument of His anger to discipline His people Israel for example, "the Assyrian, the rod of my anger, in whose hand is the club of my wrath" (Isaiah 10:5). However, once Israel repented of her evil deeds, God judged the nation or nations who had attacked her: "Woe to the Assyrian" (Isaiah 10:5).

When the leaders of Israel took advantage of their position by stealing land, God declared that He would "pour out [His] wrath on them like a flood of water" (Hosea 5:10). He wanted the leaders to realize that He was the Landlord, and to steal land is not just taking from subjects but from the Lord Himself.

There are numerous examples of how God can hate and be angry. Several times God declares His hatred toward ritual and sham in worship, where people are just going through the motions of required worship but their hearts are far from Him. He expressed Himself quite plainly in the past: "Your New Moon festivals and your appointed feasts my soul hates" (Isaiah 1:14). The remedy for this state of affairs is sharply defined: "Wash and make yourselves clean. Take your evil deeds out of my sight!

Stop doing wrong, learn to do right!" (Isaiah 1:16-17). Furthermore, He hates those who mix true worship with the false religious practices of the peoples of the Middle East: "I hate, I despise your religious feasts" (Amos 5:21). The tragedy is that the leadership in northern Israel had cut themselves off from Jerusalem and, therefore, had perverted true worship.

Neither does the New Testament minimize this attribute of God. He hates false doctrine and a detestable life-style: "You hate the practices of the Nicolaitans, which I also hate" (Revelation 2:6); "Whoever rejects the Son will not see life, for God's wrath remains on him" (John 3:36).

SEVEN FOLLIES GOD HATES (6:17-19)

THE HAUGHTY EYES (6:17*a*)

The "haughty eyes" are, literally, "eyes [that are] lifted up." In our culture, a proud person has a "lifted up" *nose*, but the Bible uses another picture to describe the superior look in Semitic culture: proud, haughty eyes.

Pride has always incurred God's hatred, and He detests it. A quick survey of Scripture demonstrates this truth. When proud Lucifer wanted to be like the Most High, he was deposed (Isaiah 14:12-15) and became God's arch-enemy. The "desire for gaining wisdom" is a temptation of pride, which Satan used to bring our first parents into ruin (Genesis 3:5), and the cost of this venture introduced sin into the human race.

A man who walks in his haughtiness will be brought "low" (29:23). The self-sufficient and prosperous wicked person who feels he is in command of every situation does not realize that his pride is really like a necklace (see discussion of 1:8-9). Someday these folks will find themselves "on slippery ground" and soon "cast" down "to ruin" (Psalm 73:3, 6, 18). Neither is the New Testament slack in the condemnation of pride: when Herod became vain and proud in his speech, and "did not give praise to God, an angel of the Lord struck him down" (Acts 12:21-23).

Humility, the opposite characteristic, leads to the acceptance of divine authority. Can we be any different than the one greater than Solomon, who, after having washed the disciples' feet, said, "I have set you an example that you should do as I have done for you" (John 13:15). Listen to God's warning concerning the folly of the haughty eyes: *The proud person and I cannot live together in this world!*

THE LYING TONGUE (6:17*b*)

A "lying tongue" is literally "a tongue of color," which speaks falsely and deceitfully and is therefore detested by God. Wisdom describes the uselessness of the lying tongue: its insinuations can last "only for a moment" (12:19), and riches obtained through its use are compared to "a fleeting vapor" that soon blows away (21:6).

The crooked tongue hates, as a rule, those it hurts (26:28) and seems to delight especially in slandering believers. God hates the liar. This is seen ever so sharply with the realization that all truth is grounded in God's own being. He is called the God of truth (Psalm 31:5*b*), and all "the works of His hands are faithful and just" (Psalm 111:7-8). When evil men open their mouths and speak lies about God's standards, they are twisting them, perverting His words, and distorting His very being. To be true to His nature, God detests this activity and will judge it.

Jesus' pointed description of Satan contrasts with God's character. Satan does not hold "to the truth for there is no truth in him"; "he is a liar and the father of lies" and of all that is false (John 8:44). When people try to mimic what Satan does, is it any wonder that God's wrath is aroused?

Each of God's children is to put "off all falsehood and speak truthfully to his neighbor" (Ephesians 4:25). The unrepentant folly of the lying tongue has eternal consequences: "the unbelieving . . . and all liars—their place will be in the fiery lake of burning sulfur" (Revelation 21:8).

MURDER (6:17c)

The world generally thinks the crime of murder should be at the top of any list of sins, but a study of crime and sin in the Bible reveals that selfishness, pride, and lies can all lead to murder. For this reason, Wisdom mentions the haughty eyes and the lying tongue before speaking of murder.

Murder is described by the phrase "hands that shed innocent blood." The emphasis is on the cold, premeditated act, or the worst possible case of manslaughter, where innocent people do not suspect harm in any way.

The relationship between blood and life is an Old Testament concept. We are told that "the life of a creature is in the blood" (Leviticus 17:11), and when the blood was poured out, life was regarded as given up or laid down. The shedding of blood, then, takes on major significance. Abel's blood on the ground cried out to God and evoked an immediate response from Him (Genesis 4:10).

But there is something even more significant about murder. The offender does not merely cause some biological process to cease. His action is also an affront against God Himself, "for in the image of God has God made man" (Genesis 9:6). Murder means, therefore, a marring of the image of God. God places the worth of the individual life on the highest possible plane, thereby stressing the dignity of man.

The value of individual life is further emphasized in that God sent His Son, His best, into the world to atone for our sins so that we could be redeemed. By such a magnanimous offer, God portrayed the great worth of humanity. What an answer to some of the ideologies of our day: Communism, which submerges the individual in the interests of the supreme state; Jean Paul Sartre, who, in his atheistic existentialism, says that when man dies he sinks into nothingness. "You shall not murder" (Exodus 20:13) declares the moral absolute. God detests murder because it is an assault upon Him.

THE SCHEMING HEART (6:18a)

The Lord detests "a heart which devises wicked schemes." Literally, wisdom describes such activity as "the heart constantly thinking [or, plowing] all kinds of schemes of wickedness." The metaphor pictures a farmer working hard to prepare the ground for planting. The teacher uses this picture to describe people hard at work, always devising the many kinds of iniquity. Hosea likewise proclaimed that "Ephraim is a trained heifer" who has "planted wickedness" and "reaped evil" (Hosea 10:11-13).

Evil thoughts well up in every person's heart, but when an individual constantly dwells on these thoughts and plans, he turns his heart into the devil's workshop. What then comes forth only reflects the utter moral depravity of the human being. We should not think that any one of us is immune. It only takes the right circumstances to demonstrate what Jeremiah declared: "The heart is deceitful above all things and beyond cure. Who can understand it?" (Jeremiah 17:9). Not all of us fall into the same traps, but "we all, like sheep, have gone astray, each of us has turned to his own way" (Isaiah 53:6).

Wisdom seeks to warn us. Our inventive faculties are to be used for the good of our fellow man, for the glory of God, and for making "the teaching about God our Savior attractive" (Titus 2:10), not for shameful and base purposes. We are not to bring other people into distress and ruin. Young people, therefore, have an extremely important lesson to learn, and wisdom wishes to drive this lesson home so as to establish a good, wholesome thought life.

Nothing is hidden from God, because all our thoughts are known to Him. A day of reckoning is coming for the man or woman who discounts God's omniscience and lets his or her mind dwell on evil thoughts continually. On that day, such people will have their thoughts projected for all to see. The New Testament reminds us that "whatever is right . . . if anything is excellent or praiseworthy —think on these things" (Philippians 4:8).

EAGERNESS TO SWIFTLY DO EVIL (6:18b)

With a picture of vivid activity wisdom describes "feet that are quick to rush into evil" (literally, "speeding feet, to run to iniquity"). A combination of verbs depicts rapid movement to perform wickedness and do evil.

Isaiah used this description in a negative way, speaking of those who "are swift to shed innocent blood" (Isaiah 59:7), which is another metaphor on the speediness or eagerness to do evil and participate in mischief making. On the other hand the psalmist uses this peculiar expression positively, describing the swift action of God's Word that "runs swiftly" (Psalm 147:15), encouraging people to do what is good.

By using the words *feet*, *path*, and *way*, wisdom talks about a person's character as he or she moves about in this world. God describes worthy people who bring forth the good tidings of peace as having "beautiful . . . feet" (Isaiah 52:7). Paul uses the same figure in Romans 10:15.

On the other hand, the one who conceives wicked schemes in his heart and whose feet carry out his evil deeds is best described as nauseating. Wisdom admonishes believers to guard the heart and to keep the feet from following evil. David himself is the example. In the affair with Bathsheba, the lust conceived in his heart swiftly led to adultery and murder. Eventually the discipline within his family was totally disrupted. James warns us of the "heart to feet circuit" (see James 1:14-15).

Truly, "the journey of a 1,000 miles begins with the first step."[2] The young person is, therefore, warned to watch that first step, being careful that it leads to a godly life-style. If not, he or she will be led down the wrong trail to where it becomes easy to be eager to do evil.

2. Old Chinese proverb.

THE FALSE WITNESS (6:19*a*)

The Lord abhors the "false witness." This goes a step farther than what has been described concerning the lying tongue (6:17). On that occasion, it was unofficial and private, though not any less distasteful. Here, however, is an official action bound to have repercussions in the lives of others.

Literally, wisdom describes this action as "one in the habit of breathing out deceptions [as] the witness of a falsehood." In some instances, a garden can be made to "breathe out *fragrance*" (Song of Solomon 4:16; NASB). But in other instances it can be just the opposite, with God breathing out His "fiery anger" (Ezekiel 21:31). A false witness is regarded as having a most odious breath, conveying accurately the putrid-smelling action God detests.

Scripture records a number of such incidents. False witnesses testified that they heard Naboth curse "both God and the king" (Ahab); as a result Naboth was "stoned to death" (1 Kings 21:13-14). A man is also a false witness when he says he has a word from God but really has no such message. Tragically, people will be led astray when they listen to false witnesses (Jeremiah 23:32). Stephen was confronted by false witnesses, and justice was perverted when they said he spoke "words of blasphemy against Moses and against God . . . against the holy place and against the law" (Acts 6:11, 13). As a result, Stephen lost his life. God takes seriously the matter of perjured testimony because moral absolutes are broken. He must judge the offender.

SPREADING STRIFE (6:19*b*)

The final folly in this list of detestable attitudes and actions is the "man who stirs up dissension among brothers." Literally, the picture is "one sending forth dissension between others" (see 6:14). There seems to be no intent to limit the term of literal brothers, since a number of circles might be in mind.

Troublemakers take delight in stirring up fights between various parties. Petty jealousies can embitter families. False rumors can undermine and divide churches. Many units of society can be broken by the troublemaker who shoots his poison of strife into the midst of his group. Strife can be stirred in a number of ways. A person can be a "tattletale" and pass along information he should have buried. Many an estrangement has taken place because someone did not have the grace to forget. Talebearing is prohibited: "Do not go about spreading slander among your people" (Leviticus 19:16).

Whole churches have been split because of misunderstandings and gossip. Worse yet is the deliberate destruction of harmony because someone enjoys an open fight. And many a dictator, pounding his lies long enough, has made people accept his propaganda, wreaking international havoc. The Hitler-Goebbels team in their National Socialist propaganda efforts in the 1930s set the stage for World War II, the death of millions, and the racial genocide of 6 million Jewish people. Diabolical are the effects of discord. God hates the troublemaker who disrupts harmony. In sharp contrast, Jesus said, "Blessed are the peacemakers" (Matthew 5:9).

For whoever finds me [wisdom] finds life
and receives favor from the Lord.
But whoever fails to find me harms himself;
all who hate me love death.

Proverbs 8:35-36

7

WISDOM AND HER RIVALS
(8:1-36; 9:1-18)

Passing from the subject of sexual immorality (chapter 5) and the theme of the follies God hates (chapter 6),
we turn from darkness to light. In places of seclusion and
darkness, Satan lurks to enslave, and he works through
questionable attitudes and activities to destroy man's
soul. Now, however, we approach the wide vistas of freedom where God wants to enrich everyone who seeks Him.
Wisdom has her legitimate, tempting delights for the best
experiences in life.

Proverbs 8:1-5 contains a further contrast to that of
the temptress in Proverbs 7:1-27 and the husband's fury
toward the one who committed adultery with his wife in
6:30-35. The pleasures of sin can be enjoyed for a short
while, but in the end its fruit is bitter. In particular, the
Mosaic constitution directed that no sacrifices were available for immorality. Furthermore, to insure Israel's sacred
position before the Lord, the community was to exact the
death penalty for such flagrant sin. In Proverbs 8, wisdom
issues her call out in the open (see 1:20-27). She occupies
the most conspicuous sites, calling to all classes of people:

to the men of status (8:4), as well as to the inexperienced and fools (8:5).

THE VALUES OF WISDOM (8:1-11)

The offer of the values of wisdom is for whoever will listen. Never does godly wisdom appeal only to the select few. As many as will respond and commit themselves can enjoy everything wisdom offers.

Even as the New Testament believer has the privilege of laying hold of "every spiritual blessing in Christ" (Ephesians 1:3), so believers in both Testament eras have been able to secure the blessings of wisdom. She crowns her willing adherents with values that, at the least, win the grudging admiration of worldly people. Certainly, the person who lives wisdom's values merits the greatest praise of God.

The wise disciple learns "worthy things to say," and his lips "speak what is right" (8:6). The naive can have the high privilege of speaking "what is true" with words that "are just" (8:8a). What else could be more commendable amidst a people who exhibit questionable, and even deplorable, moral values? Indeed, all of wisdom's words "are right" (or straightforward) to her disciples, for they practice discernment; her words "are faultless to those who have knowledge" (8:9). The important aspect in verse 9 is the testing of God's truth; those who are willing to try it out will find knowledge that is true. As the wise disciple actively responds to wisdom's constant call and quest, seeking and searching out her discernment and knowledge, the value of what is just and right will be keenly appreciated along the paths of wisdom.

The values of wisdom are worth more than "silver," "gold," and "rubies." In fact, nothing one desires "can compare with her" (8:10-11). (See again the discussion of 3:14-15.) The morals of worldly people clash sharply with what is valuable from God's point of view; only wisdom offers what is most necessary for a worry-free life on earth. Believers in the Old Testament era knew these truths well, even as we can know them today.

THOSE WHO RECEIVE THE REWARDS OF WISDOM (8:12-21)

In 8:1-11 the godly teacher has been extolling the values of wisdom. But from 8:12 onward wisdom personified speaks for herself concerning rewards and benefits shared with those who receive her.

Wisdom alone can provide the right "counsel" and advice to those in doubt. She is the one who gives "sound judgment" or "practical sense" to those who follow her (8:14a). When "kings reign," "rulers make laws," "princes govern," and "nobles . . . rule" in an acceptable manner, they do so only because they have sought godly wisdom (8:15-16). The glory of a nation is enhanced when its leadership is not ashamed to ask for and use what wisdom provides. Many are the rulers who govern nations abominably, and God has His way of repudiating them and their people when they reject wisdom's guidelines (Hosea 8:4).

Wisdom reveals her deepest feelings when she adds, "I love those who love me" (8:17a), and her solemn promise is that "those who seek me find me" (8:17b). The man who honestly seeks godly guidance in the affairs of life will certainly enjoy access to wisdom. In the New Testament version of Proverbs, James also reflects on this offer to those lacking in wisdom: "If any of you lacks wisdom, he should ask God, who gives generously to all without finding fault, and it will be given to him" (James 1:5).

Wisdom mentions the rewards she eagerly desires to share with those who follow her. Some are material, but the primary emphasis is on the immaterial. If people have material gifts—riches, wealth and prosperity, fine gold, choice silver, wealth, and full treasuries (8:18, 19, 21)—it is only because they exercise a wise use of the gift of wisdom. She walks "in the way of righteousness, along the paths of justice, bestowing wealth on those who love" her (8:20-21a). The presence of riches in Israel under the Mosaic constitution was a sure sign that believers or national leaders had established a distinct priority in their use of godly wisdom.

We need, however, to remember the distinction between Old and New Testament economies regarding material blessings—they are not necessarily promised for today (see 3:9-10). The principle remains the same, however, in terms of *spiritual* blessings as we use wisdom wisely. Those who receive the rewards of wisdom have learned how to enjoy genuine peace in the soul.

WISDOM IN THE CREATION (8:22-31)

Wisdom proceeds now to a new and loftier claim in her discourse, describing her exalted role in the creation of the entire universe. We know that "in the beginning God created the heavens and the earth" (Genesis 1:1). In what sense, therefore, was wisdom, personified as a person, involved in the creation? This peculiarity will be considered both here and in 8:32-36 where wisdom and the Messiah are related.

A number of claims are made by wisdom. She is older than the cosmos: "I was appointed from eternity, from the beginning, before the world began" (8:23). She was already in existence when the heavens were established: "I was there when he set the heavens in place" (8:27a). Likewise, wisdom was already present when the earth was created ("before the world began"; 8:23b) and, in fact, already existed prior to the establishment of any order on the earth —its oceans, "springs abounding with water," mountains, dust, fields, the boundary of the sea, and its foundation (8:24-26, 29). She was the "craftsman" in consultation with God (8:30a), "filled with delight day after day, rejoicing always in His presence" as His workmanship was demonstrated (8:30b-c). Wisdom rejoices "in his whole world" (lit., "playing in the habitable world of the earth"; 8:31a), a reference to the delight wisdom has with living creatures who live on the earth. In particular, she takes delight "in mankind" (8:31b), which is the crown of creation, especially so when wisdom becomes man's guide in all the affairs of his life.

But when did wisdom first appear? The answer hinges on how we translate and understand 8:22. The

King James, the *New American Standard Bible,* and the *New International Version*'s footnote all translate the passage as "The Lord possessed me." Other variants are "The Lord created me" (RSV*), "The Lord brought me forth" (NIV†), and "The Lord made me" (The Jewish Publication Society, vol. II, 1955). The best evangelical opinion is against any suggestion of creation; in other words, one must not speak of the creation of wisdom at any point in history. Wisdom cannot be separated from any acceptable consideration of the very being of God, who is "the only [wise, added in a number of versions] God" (1 Timothy 1:17). She is, therefore, like Him "from everlasting to everlasting" (Psalm 90:2).

We need to understand more fully, however, what is meant when 8:22 describes wisdom as being "brought . . . forth." The context suggests the clue for further information. In 8:23 wisdom declares, "I was appointed," and in 8:24-25 she says twice, "I was given birth." In the one instance, the emphasis is on an appointment in office, while in the other reference is made to a kind of "birth." Since wisdom is linked to an eternal God, it is best to see her (1) as always existing, and then (2) appointed and brought forth for a ministry in the creation process.

Wisdom also has her function in sustaining the universe, or cosmos, as well as in providing guidance for mankind. For wisdom to say, therefore, "The Lord brought me forth" (or, possessed me), means that God made use of a wisdom already present in His very being, and by wisdom, as God possessed her, the universe came into existence.

A deep mystery surrounds the meaning of the words "possessed," "appointed," and "given birth." From the New Testament, we know that Messiah the Son was "the firstborn over all creation. For by Him all things were created . . . and in Him all things hold together" (Colossians 1:15-17). Paul declares that in Him "are hidden all the treasures of wisdom and knowledge" (Colossians 2:3),

* *Revised Standard Version.*
† *New International Version.*

while John describes the Son as "the ruler of God's creation" (Revelation 3:14). Because Jesus the Messiah has all the attributes wisdom exhibited in 8:22-25—involvement in creation, sustaining the creation, and possessing wisdom—we could say that, since wisdom does not exist independently of the Godhead, she is found *in* the living Word, Jesus the Messiah. Obviously, this passage is most difficult to understand, but we should at least see that wisdom had her part in the creation process, and that further revelation in the New Testament indicates that she actually is in the Messiah, who was really the agent of creation. The more complete revelation of the Son in the New Testament helps us to grasp better the work of wisdom in 8:22-25.

A MATTER OF LIFE AND DEATH (8:32-36)

Having noted the peculiar position and function of wisdom in creation, we are confronted by her concluding command to listen to her plea. Because she was involved in the creation process (particularly man), she claims her right to be heard. Twice she commands men and women to "listen" (8:32-33); and she promises blessings to the person who "listens" (lit., "continues to listen"; 8:34).

If men or women will take the time to hear what wisdom has to say, they can have joy unspeakable; they will be twice "blessed" (8:32, 34). These are not vain words, describing humanly induced "religious" feelings; rather, her blessings reflect a genuine inflow from God who provides genuine joy for the obedient heart and soul. A believer can continually receive "favor from the Lord" (8:35*b*) and be the object of His delight, and God will be well pleased with him.

A compelling reason reminds the believer to listen to moral discipline and not even begin to "ignore [or, neglect] it" (8:33*b*). The disciples of wisdom have a mandate not to doze or be careless with what she desires to teach them; instead, they must watch "daily at [her] doors, waiting at [her] doorway" (8:34*b-c*). For the assurance has been that those who seek wisdom earnestly will find her

(8:17b). Now we are also told that when we find her, we find life (8:35a).

God's people have the assurance of a full and happy life on earth, but the ultimate experience is sweet fellowship and communion with the Lord forever. David had the same promise from wisdom. He recited all the blessings available to him in this life: lacking "nothing" (Psalm 23:1a); lying "down in green pastures" (Psalm 23:2a); being led "beside quiet waters" (Psalm 23:2b); fearing "no evil" (Psalm 23:4b); "comfort" (Psalm 23:4e); a table loaded with benefits (Psalm 23:5a); a head anointed with oil and possessing an overflowing cup (Psalm 23:5b-c); and knowing God's goodness and love (Psalm 23:6a). But in addition to all his material blessings, David could also reflect confidently on wisdom's promise regarding eternity: "I will dwell in the house of the Lord forever" (Psalm 23:6b).

But what will happen to the person who "fails to find" wisdom (8:36a)? The Hebrew word behind "fails" is the basic word for "sin" or "missing the mark." Literally, the passage is, "Whoever is continually sinning against me [or, missing me] wrongs his own soul." Furthermore, the parallel idea in the second line of the verse is that "all who make a practice of hating me love death" (8:36b). The person who turns his back on wisdom's pleas will be miserable in his or her soul. But an even worse prospect is to scorn wisdom's advice, for this results in an eternal spiritual death.

A further parallel is found in 8:35a. Wisdom offers life to those who listen to her, and the Son Himself likewise offers "life" (John 5:40) because "in Him" is "life" (John 1:4). The Son proclaimed on still another occasion, "If a man keeps my word, he will never see death" (John 8:51).

Wisdom appears in the book of Proverbs many times as a person who is separate from God, but a proper understanding of her being and function is that she is very much a part of who God is. Wisdom herself is *not* God, but she acts and speaks as a person much like God does. The more complete revelation is in the Son incarnate.

Therefore, wisdom is identified with the Son. Because wisdom's words and appeals have a right to be heard in the Old Testament, the Son will likewise, on the basis of who He is, reflect in the New Testament all that wisdom has offered. Be careful with wisdom. It is a matter of life and death and not to be trifled with.

WISDOM'S BLESSED BANQUET (9:1-6)

In a new, striking scene, wisdom now appears as a gracious hostess who has prepared a sumptuous banquet for numerous guests she expects to entertain.

Note the *preparations*: "wisdom has built her house" (9:1a). The structure is elaborate with its "seven pillars" (9:1b), reflecting the typical architecture of Middle Eastern culture. Special care has been taken in slaughtering, dressing, and preparing "her meat" (9:2a), all for the purpose of delighting the taste of a gourmet. "Her wine" has been carefully flavored with the best of spices (Song of Solomon 8:2). The table has been elegantly set with dishes for a state occasion that reflects the exquisite taste of the hostess (9:2b). With everything in readiness, wisdom now sends "out her maids," or attendants: "and she calls from the highest point of the city" (9:3b), from the most prominent places, with invitations to the lavish feast.

Note the *guests' privileges* as this gracious, elegant hostess extends invitations through attractive maidens for all who will come to her elaborate banquet. One might think that only the most elite of society would be welcomed. Instead, her privileged guests are the "simple" and inexperienced; her favored company are "those who lack judgment [lit., lack heart]" (9:4). These are the folk who, recognizing their hunger for wisdom's banquet, have the high privilege of savoring the food and quaffing the wine that wisdom has prepared (9:5). Those who are stuffed with their own self-sufficiency will never appreciate or enjoy what wisdom has to offer at her banquet.

Note, however, the *guests' responsibilities*. Every guest of a host or hostess has certain responsibilities that cannot be violated, or he or she will overstep the boundary of proper behavior. Wisdom's banquet guests are to leave their "simple ways" (9:6a) of moral inexperience and to "walk in the way of understanding [or, discernment and moral discrimination] (9:6b).

All of this imagery is for the purpose of making wisdom's offers attractive, and what she has to offer is available to all. Her food for thought and our will to act and receive it are features that will give us the abundant, blessed life. How can anyone be so ungrateful as to refuse the invitation to wisdom's blessed banquet?

DECISIONS LEAD TO DESTINIES (9:7-12)

The central section of Proverbs 9 lies between two different kinds of invitations. The choice in selecting one or the other is important for every person because it leads to two different destinies. Those who respond to wisdom's maidens and choose her gracious banquet, though lacking in understanding and moral experience, will soon see a change in themselves. They will be known as wise, because wisdom imbues the company at her table with altogether new qualities. The wise man who sits at wisdom's banquet "will be wiser still" (9:9a). Here is a distinct contrast: worldly knowledge by itself tends to inflate a person's ego, making him so self-sufficient and self-reliant that he stops learning altogether.

The "wise man" makes it a habit to accept "rebuke," (the correction offered by wisdom, his hostess) and will love her because he knows she has his best interests in her heart. He humbly acknowledges his inexperience and lack of understanding (9:4). With "the fear of the Lord" (9:10a) in his or her heart, a person enjoys the happiest experiences of life in the midst of her blessings.

Those who reject wisdom's invitation are viewed as mockers. They see no need to attend wisdom's banquet, and, upon being invited, they will offer only insult: "Whoever corrects a mocker invites insult" (9:7a). Wisdom's maids blush with shame from this abuse. The rebel is crude: "Whoever rebukes a wicked man incurs abuse" (9:7b), and he thereby questions the queenly character of wisdom and makes her as one of the common women of the street.

It is useless to correct a committed mocker because he will react violently and despise correction: "Do not rebuke a mocker or he will hate you" (9:8*a*). How different is this reaction from the one who is willing to accept wisdom's invitation and help.

A person doesn't insult and shame such gracious offers without suffering the consequences. Such a scoffer of wisdom will eventually bear his own disgrace: "If you are a mocker, you alone will suffer" (9:12*b*). Life's decisions lead to lasting destinies.

<h2 style="text-align:center">Folly's Cursed Crumbs (9:13-18)</h2>

Folly, too, is pictured as a woman, literally, as "the foolish woman" (9:13*a*). No greater contrast can be found than that of folly and wisdom.

The woman of folly, in contrast to the gracious hostess of wisdom, is "loud, undisciplined and without knowledge [lit., she knows not what]" (9:13). She has made no preparation to entertain. She is repugnant, repulsive, and "sits at the door of her house" (9:14*a*) to seduce passers-by. In this sense, she acts like a prostitute, and a very common one at that. She is a contrast to wisdom's gracious invitation issued through her handmaidens. Folly makes her own appeal, but she lacks refined dignity and the aesthetic quality that characterizes wisdom.

Folly, too, like wisdom, invites the simple and inexperienced. "'Let all who are simple come in here!' she shouts to those who lack judgment [lit., lack heart]" (9:16; see also 9:4). But what does she offer her guests? Only "stolen water" and "food eaten in secret" (9:17). Under this imagery she offers the kind of life that feeds the sensual nature of man. In fact, she thinks this bill of fare is so desirable that she says the "stolen water is sweet" and her food "delicious" (9:17).

Folly, however, does not even begin to satisfy the heart hunger of man, and offers nothing to slake the thirst of the soul. There is nothing at her table to help the morally inexperienced progress in discernment, understanding, and spiritual maturity. All folly has to offer are some stale crumbs and scummy water.

Furthermore, folly says nothing of the death that relentlessly dogs the one who makes a habit of eating from this menu. Those who persist will one day find out that in folly's house is the poison of darkness. The saying is that "these wicked are accounted as dead even while alive," because "little do" folly's guests "know that the dead are there" in her house (9:18a). Those who attend her banquet are already "in the depths of the grave [lit., *sheol*]" (9:18b).

For guests feeding on what folly has to offer, life becomes a dismal experience and death a time of horror. Eternity will yawn open to snatch its foolish victims, and they will be separated from the Lord forever and ever. How can anyone be so blind as to choose the consequences of such a revolting invitation to partake of folly's cursed crumbs?

To a man belong the plans of the heart,
but from the LORD comes the reply of the tongue.
All a man's ways seem innocent to him,
but motives are weighed by the LORD.
Commit to the LORD whatever you do,
and your plans will succeed.

Proverbs 16:1-3

8

GOD AND MAN

Once beyond Proverbs 9, the book does not lend itself
to a continuous outline, except for groups of couplets
dealing with a specific topic in a few chapters. It is best,
therefore, to select some of the more prominent topics in
these chapters to provide an extremely valuable guide for
everyday living and godly life-style.

Some of the topics that should prove most interesting
and helpful are as follows: God and man; the believer and
his emotions; human relationships in families and society; speech, laziness, and folly; and a matter of life and
death. In this chapter we discover what Proverbs has to
say regarding the relationship between man and God
through God's various names.

GOD AND A PRACTICAL ETHIC

Two candidates in a presidential race had to resign,
one because of a relationship with another woman and the
other because of untruthful exaggeration and plagiarism
in his speeches. While such news was depressing, the situation became even worse when a third candidate was in-
terviewed by reporters. He claimed that the media was

focusing on the nonessentials and overlooking the primary issues of a presidential campaign.

What has happened to presidential candidates to give them such little sense as to what constitutes basic morality? The sad fact is that officials, and the people who support them, seem to have lost the meaning of a God-given ethic. Such ethics are not conditioned by society; rather, they are proclaimed by the holy God of the Scriptures. Because He is holy and righteous, we have an absolute ethical standard by which leaders can be judged today and by which all people will one day be held accountable.

The book of Proverbs has an ethic for everyday life based upon the holiness and righteousness of God. From what we have seen already in the Introduction, the function of the wise man was to develop a practical wisdom based on God's revelation. The Lord is interested in practical affairs so that His righteousness can be translated into so-called secular pursuits: the marketplace, where "the Lord abhors dishonest scales, but accurate weights are His delight" (11:1); caring for the poor, for "he who is kind to the poor lends to the Lord" (19:17a); the rights of the underprivileged, for "the Lord . . . keeps the widow's boundaries intact" (15:25).

The wisdom of Proverbs must be at the foundation of every aspect of national life, including ambitious pursuits by men who wish to attain the presidency or serve in any branch of government. God desires that everyone live morally, recognizing that He is holy. He cannot give His approval to those who flout His standards.

By far, the most frequent name for God in the book of Proverbs is "LORD" (*Yahweh*), appearing some ninety-six times. We shall note how this particular name relates to everyday life. There are three other names for God and His relationship to man: *El* or God; *Eloha, Elohim*; and Holy One. The various names for man are also interesting: *'adam*, as a part of humanity; *enosh*, which depicts man's lowliness and insignificance; and *gever*, which pictures the warrior or mighty one.

THE LORD (*YAHWEH*) AND MAN

Whatever we attempt to derive from the root meaning of *Yahweh*, this name describes God as the personal, living God who delivered Israel from Egypt. The Lord revealed Himself to Moses, declaring, "I am the Lord and I will bring you out from under the yoke of the Egyptians" (Exodus 6:6). In a general sense, therefore, *Yahweh* is the covenant name of God. It relates to Israel's deliverance from Egypt, God's presence at Sinai, where He gave His people the law, and His eventual establishment of them in the land of Canaan.

Yet, even though the revelation of *Yahweh* throughout the book of Proverbs is conditioned and colored from a national point of view, the wisdom present in this book has a universal character, appealing to all men everywhere, in many ages and in many countries. For that reason, the Lord can also give believers today sound wisdom to live a godly life-style. The wisdom expressed in Proverbs can also be a guide to unbelievers if they wish to be sensitive to the Lord's desires; but if not, this very wisdom becomes a condemnation of their evil conduct.

Some fifteen areas exist in the book of Proverbs wherein *Yahweh* addresses Himself to man, providing for him what is the most desirable life-style. We shall begin with the themes that have the greatest number of passages and then proceed to the subjects employing the least number of verses.

THE FEAR OF THE LORD

This theme appears in most of the verses that relate to the name *Yahweh*. We have already discussed what it means to have a fear for the Lord (1:7, 29; 2:5; 3:7; 8:13; 9:10). Further uses of this phrase occur some eighteen times in chapters 10-31.

How to live long and be upright. When a person fears the Lord, he or she "adds length to life" (10:27a). By contrast, those who do not have any fear for Him will soon realize that "the years of the wicked are cut short"

(10:27*b*). It may be true, according to some biologists, that the length of a person's life is already determined in his or her genes from birth. On the other hand, longevity can also be determined by individual conduct, and if one chooses not to fear the Lord, life can be cut short.

Those who fear the Lord, therefore, walk uprightly before Him (14:2*a*). To ignore or even deliberately set out to reject God's wisdom signifies that a person's "ways are devious" and that such people despise Him (14:2*b*). We have far too many today, even in high places, whose ways are perverted because they do not understand God's righteousness.

The Lord is our protection. The Lord is a God of love and seeks to assure His own of His care and concern. He will be to those who fear Him a "secure fortress, and for his children it will be a refuge" (14:26). The Lord protects His own people who fear Him and are faithful to Him. In addition, "the fear of the Lord is a fountain of life, turning a man from the snares of death" (14:27). We shall yet discuss the meaning of "the fountain of life" in chapter 12, but even now we note that the wisdom of God is life, and for those who fear the Lord He is light and life.

Better to be calm than anxious. In a materialistic society, particularly in the West, the tragedy of misplaced confidence is a crushing load. What has the wealthy person gained if, after he piles up his millions of dollars, he only realizes that it does not provide satisfaction? Instead, such a person will find himself in "turmoil," or disturbed and anxious. The contrast is clear and sharp: wisdom declares, "Better a little with the fear of the Lord" (15:16) because it will yield a calm security for the man or woman of faith.

As an antidote to the feverish search for more and more things, the book of Proverbs reminds us: "The fear of the Lord teaches [or, instructs, disciplines] a man wisdom, and humility comes before honor" (15:33). Of much greater wealth is God's discipline or instruction taught by a godly fear of Him than all the money or prestige in this world. God's glory and honor are reserved for those who have established priorities in their lives in order to be humble men and women.

Should we envy the prosperous wicked? The godly person understands that "through the fear of the Lord a man avoids evil" (16:6b). The Hebrew word for "evil," *ra'*, can also mean any kind of misfortune. Therefore, when a person bases his or her moral conduct on the fear of the Lord, he or she will avoid many problems.

The people of Israel were promised material blessings. This included good health, not only for themselves but also for their flocks. Nevertheless, disconcerting, harrying experiences occurred even in Old Testament times. Asaph was troubled with the prosperity of the wicked, even envying them for their freedom from "the burdens common to man" (Psalm 73:5a). Not until he "entered the sanctuary of God" did he understand "their final destiny" (Psalm 73:17). Even if riches were gained wrongfully, the Lord had His way of evening out the score.

Believers under the New Covenant are not necessarily promised physical blessings. To some extent, as we live a devout life-style, we will be spared some of the social diseases that plague promiscuous people. The point, however, is that when we do suffer misfortune our hope is in the Lord. We are to "endure hardship as discipline" because "God is treating [us] as sons" (Hebrews 12:7). In the midst of our difficulties, we are to triumphantly strengthen the "feeble arms and weak knees" (Hebrews 12:12).

"Humility and the fear of the Lord bring wealth and honor and life" (22:4; see also 14:26). From an Old Testament point of view, such a promise is based upon the stipulation outlined in the Mosaic constitution for material blessings. A rabbinic proverb is based upon this verse: "'The fear of the Lord,' which wisdom makes the crown of the head, humility makes the imprint of the feet." Its implications go beyond mere material things: the pious person who responds to the fear of the Lord will have knowledge and wisdom to lay hold of eternal life.

Make careful decisions. Wisdom seeks to encourage believers not to "envy sinners, but always be zealous for the fear of the Lord" (23:17). This verse might be paraphrased in this way: do not envy sinners, but really envy those who are in the fear of the Lord. While many in our society today live out their days coveting what others have, wisdom asks a pointed question: "Why should our lives be caught up with materialism, the grab for power simply for personal gain, and trampling over others with no thought or concern for the less fortunate?" The wisdom and knowledge that can be learned from the fear of the Lord is so much better than the frustration of an ungodly ambition. But if the Lord does put a believer in a position of authority, he will be a blessing to the people he serves.

Should we always obey the government? The last statement of this theme encourages people both to "fear the Lord and the king" (24:21). The king or any governmental authority is actually God's representative, and, generally, wisdom directs His charge to give honor to whom honor is due, including governmental authorities. Even though at times government leaders can become evil, that is no excuse to mount a rebellion.

Times and circumstances arise, however, when we can no longer yield our allegiance to governmental authorities: when we are challenged regarding our faith, and when a government becomes completely immoral. In the first instance, Peter proclaimed to the Sanhedrin, "We must obey God rather than men!" (Acts 5:29). Peter leaves no doubt that government has no right to control our thought life. In the latter sense, no government has the right to kill people because of who they are, as when the Nazis set out to kill all Jewish people in Europe. Solomon reminds us again to "obey the king's command . . . because you took an oath before God" (Ecclesiastes 8:2). But occasions will arise because of man's extreme immorality when a government must be overthrown: "For there is a proper time and procedure for every matter, though a man's misery weighs heavily upon him" (Ecclesiastes 8:6). Wisdom recognizes those special times when we cannot be obedient to completely immoral ideology and evil government officials, but such circumstances may exact a heavy toll.

OMNISCIENCE, CREATOR, AND PURPOSE

An emphasis almost equally important to the fear of
the Lord is that God is all-knowing, has purpose in everything He does, and must certainly be regarded as the Creator. While this emphasis appears once in 5:21, it occurs in
chapters 10-31 some seventeen times.

The Lord knows man's decisions and experiences.
Significant is the observation by wisdom that "the eyes of
the Lord are everywhere, keeping watch on the wicked
and the good" (15:3). God keeps watch in the same sense
that the prophet earnestly sought to be the spiritual guide
of the people (Ezekiel 3:17). Nothing escapes God's attention from His front row seat in heaven; He sees how the
wicked plot their evil schemes and speak detestable lies;
at the same time He quietly approves the deeds of believers. Similarly "Death and Destruction lie open before the
Lord—how much more the hearts of men!" (15:11). If
these remote and mysterious places are known to God,
how much more does He know men's hearts and all the
thoughts hidden in them (Jeremiah 17:9, 10)?

Good people can also suffer the loss of their health or
finances, or they are heartbroken when they have to care
for their sick or handicapped children. God is not obliv-
ious to such trials, and at the proper moment He will reward those who remain faithful in the midst of their
trying circumstances.

*The Lord is our strength, but He also checks our mo-
tives.* Depending on a person's disposition, he either plans
to make the right choices to do good or schemes to commit evil: "To a man belongs the plans of the heart [lit., the
preparations of the heart]" (16:1). The picture evoked by
"plan" or "preparations" is that of a "row of soldiers" as
they plan for battle; similarly, man's plans are weighed
one against the other. However man may plan, only "from
the Lord comes the reply of the tongue" (16:1*b*). God
alone enables an individual to bring his plans to comple-
tion. A person may think he is in charge of everything he
decides, even his destiny, but he does not realize that only
the Lord enables him to do what he plans.

A "man's ways seem innocent to him, but motives are weighed by the Lord" (16:2). Society today seems so smug and satisfied with their ideas. Women pronounce confidently that their body belongs to them and that abortion should be an acceptable procedure. Homosexuals promote their life-style as a legitimate alternative. Materialists advocate greed as an acceptable ethic. Relativist educators seek the destruction of traditional morality. But false ideology, priorities, and motives are probed by God and judged accordingly.

The Lord establishes the rules. The Lord, our Creator, established His decrees to govern His comprehensive plan for the operation of the world. When a believer has a fear of the Lord and seeks to work in harmony with God's purposes and decrees, he will receive God's blessing and enjoy bliss in His presence for all eternity. Conversely, however, when the wicked have nothing to do with the Lord, even despising Him and ignoring His decrees, they will one day come to "a day of disaster" (16:4*b*). Man has a free will, but if he chooses to go the wrong way, he is destined to suffer punishment at the hands of God.

The Lord knows what He is doing. The purposes and providence of the Lord are a most important emphasis and are seen in many ways. At times lots were drawn to determine His will: "The lot is cast into the lap, but its every decision is from the Lord" (16:33). People could determine the purposes of the Lord because the result was not accidental but actually determined by Him. In such a manner, Achan was separated from all the clans and his family because he chose to disobey God regarding the "devoted things" (Joshua 7:14-15). Due to the lack of a fuller revelation to determine the will of God, God permitted the casting of lots and the use of the *Urim* and *Thummim* to determine His will.

In another illustration of how "the Lord tests the heart" (17:3*b*), wisdom points out that "the crucible for silver and the furnace for gold" (17:3*a*) are means for refining these metals to insure their purity. Gold is purified by repeatedly heating it to its boiling point and then skimming off the slag or impurity rising to the surface. People highly value gold that has been repeatedly purified. In the same way, the Lord tests the believer's character, enabling him to do His perfect will. Moses began his ministry by being trained in all the wisdom of the Egyptians. For the Lord to use this man, however, he had to be shunted into the desert for forty years, where he became a simple shepherd who knew how to carefully care for his sheep. He learned how to be humble before the Lord, who then entrusted him with the care of His people Israel. Those who wish to be used of the Lord will have to endure some time of difficult training.

The Lord has given us "ears that hear and eyes that see" (20:12a), which are the most important faculties for determining human knowledge. Man is endowed with great potential for good, but we need to be careful how we use our ears and eyes and so be accountable to the Lord who "has made them both" (20:12b; see also Psalm 94:9).

A major provision of God's purpose and providence is that "a man's steps are directed by the Lord." But the second line of the antithetic parallel passage is a question: "How then can anyone understand his own way?" (20:24). The point is that, if the wisdom of God directs a man's steps, how can a man say that he has no guidance for this world's affairs? How can he dare to make his own plans for everything he will do? The point of the question in the passage actually demands a negative reply, because wisdom makes plain that when she directs a person's life, her guidance will be in accordance with the Word of God, wherein is revealed His will.

Wisdom pointedly reminds us that, through the providence of God, kings and all government officials are controlled by Him: "The king's heart is in the hand of the Lord; He directs it like a water course wherever He pleases" (21:1). Even as the farmer digs irrigation ditches for water to pass through the most advantageous places to water his crops, so likewise the heart of the king is in actuality the means by which the Lord rules. In no way does it imply that the king or government official has no mind of his own. But even as human authority has been sanctioned by God, they are to act as His regents.

In some cases officials may become so corrupt that God has to, in His providential rule, remove such evil people from their offices. Such a case is recorded in the book of Esther. Haman schemed to do harm to Mordecai, but God had His ways of upsetting Haman's plots. The king could not sleep on the night after the gallows had been built for Mordecai's execution. So to induce slumber, he "ordered the book of the Chronicles . . . be brought in and read to him. It was found recorded there that Mordecai had exposed . . . two of the king's officers . . . who had conspired to assassinate" the king (Esther 6:1-2). The rest becomes divine irony when Haman, the man who had intended evil against Mordecai, now had to lead him through the streets in a victory parade, proclaiming his greatness (Esther 6:11). In time God rid Himself of Haman, who was not fit to continue in his office as a government official. In His providence and omniscience, God can use strange means to accomplish His purposes.

People may fight their battles and plan their grandiose schemes, but if they do not reflect the purpose of God, they will only fail. Therefore, "there is no wisdom, no insight, no plan that can succeed against the Lord. The horse is made ready for the day of battle, but victory rests with the Lord" (21:30-31). How can human wisdom compare with the wisdom of God? Even though man can plan to fight battles, without God there will be no victory. Because of the pervasive influence of humanism today, government officials and leaders think that they, as the captains of their own destinies, can lead their nations to human paradise. They will only rue the day, however, when they realize that the Lord is in control and that His providence cannot be set aside or His purposes thwarted.

All are equal before God. They may be rich or they may be poor, but they "have this in common: the Lord is the Maker of them all" (22:2). God does not delight in keeping some people poor and, by some strange quirk of His providence, making others rich. The passage should be taken at face value. The rich person is no better off because he has great wealth; he ranks on the same level before God as the poor person. A person may be so poor that he or she has hardly anything to eat, but before God he has standing equal to the mighty and wealthy.

ABHOR, DETEST

Another important theme of great consequence is how the Lord detests many features of man's conduct in everyday life. We shall discuss this theme further in chapter 9, but it also figures prominently in the relationship between man and the Lord.

The Lord abhors questionable business ethics. Wisdom pointedly warns the merchants in the marketplace, declaring that they must be accountable in their business ethics: "The Lord abhors dishonest scales, but accurate weights are His delight" (11:1). The Mosaic Constitution prohibited the use of false weights and measures (Leviticus 19:35-36; Deuteronomy 25:13-15). Likewise, the prophets, repeatedly reflecting Moses' directive, warned Israel of this violation of God's righteousness (Amos 8:5; Ezekiel 45:20; Micah 6:11). God wants honesty at every level of life, and particularly in places of commerce so that people will not be cheated (see also 16:11; 20:10, 23 for similar statements). In the rabbinic instructions, people were prohibited from possessing false weights and measures, even though they may never be used.

The Lord detests the perverse man. Nothing disgusts the Lord more than people who are perverse, thinking and acting contrary to His righteousness: "The Lord detests men of perverse hearts but He delights in those whose ways are blameless" (11:20). The perverse are to be shunned, particularly by believers. Liars are also condemned because God "detests lying lips, but He delights in men who are truthful [lit., those who act in faithfulness]" (12:22). The believer who acts in faithfulness to the wisdom provided by God will speak the truth.

The New Testament similarly reflects how the Lord feels toward those who are perverse. He not only detests liars but will also judge and consign them to their place "in the fiery lake of burning sulfur" (Revelation 21:8). The commandments are not only a vital part of the Mosaic Constitution, they also have an important place in the New Covenant. Jesus referred to all of them, as recorded in the gospels, whereas Paul referred to nine of the ten.

The apostle to the Gentiles and other writers of the New Testament used the commandments to reflect the absolute righteousness of God. Morals are not to be considered relative, allowing everyone to do what is right in his own eyes. Morals that relate to conduct must be seen as fixed and true, and they judge all actions of men by a righteous standard. Therefore, when anyone transgresses any one of the commandments, as for example, unbelievers who are liars, he will be held accountable for his actions. Unbelievers will end up in a lost eternity and be judged for their evil deeds (Revelation 20:12, 15).

Be careful how you worship. The list continues to describe what the Lord abhors: He "detests the sacrifice of the wicked, but the prayer of the upright pleases Him" (15:8). Many had a habit of going through the motions of offering their sacrifices in accordance with the Constitution, but their hearts were far removed from God's will or way. God detests a ritualistic worship where the heart is not changed at all: "Stop bringing meaningless offerings! Your incense is detestable to Me. . . . Your New Moon festivals and your appointed feasts My soul hates" (Isaiah 1:13-14). Instead, He seeks to reason with the wicked that they "wash and make" themselves clean and actually pleads, "Come now, let us reason together" (Isaiah 1:16, 18). The Lord desires righteousness and does not hesitate to express His innermost feelings for what is evil.

Choices come from the heart. The Lord also "detests the way of the wicked but loves those who pursue righteousness" (15:9). He wants people to have a persistent inner desire to pursue righteousness with a corresponding outward action to follow through in doing what is right. The parallel in 15:9 suggests a strong contrast between the wicked and the righteous, but wisdom is gracious, not desiring to write off the wicked without giving them opportunity to respond.

The real problem of wrong-doing stems from the heart: "The Lord detests the thoughts of the wicked" (15:26*a*). He knows how they inwardly scheme and plan from their wrong motives. More to be desired, however, are the thoughts "of the pure" who "are pleasing to Him" (15:26*b*).

We have already noted how God hates the haughty eyes (5:17). But the Lord also "detests all the proud of heart. Be sure of this: they will not go unpunished" (16:5). The "proud of heart" refuse to submit to God and His Word. Therefore, these arrogant folk will not be spared His angry judgment. The Lord and the proud man cannot live together in the same universe.

Be truthful. Finally, wisdom tragically describes this topsy-turvy world of questionable morals when justice is miscarried in the courts: the guilty are acquitted and the innocent condemned, which is a miserable state of affairs. The Mosaic Constitution explicitly states that judges and officials were to "judge the people fairly." They were not to "pervert justice or show partiality." Specifically, they were never to "accept a bribe, for a bribe blinds the eyes of the wise and twists the words of the righteous" (Deuteronomy 16:18-19). The point is that every Israeli and alien, poor and rich, was considered *equal* before the Law. Each one was to receive the same justice, and if a person was guilty, he was to be condemned; if someone was charged falsely, he was to be acquitted. The wisdom in Proverbs builds on what the Mosaic Constitution already declared. Therefore, the Lord decries any miscarriage of justice.

Truth-telling is an ethic all people understand because each one is made in the image of God. But when someone deliberately chooses contrary to what he knows to be right, he stands condemned before the Lord. Tragically, people are free for the present time to make choices that repulse God's very being. But such wicked people will not long enjoy their freedom. God knows how to act at just the right moment to curb evil and rectify the mess mankind is prone to make when he no longer is guided by wisdom in the Word of the Lord.

HONOR, FAVOR, BLESSINGS

God detests wickedness and arrogance. But many are the recipients of His honor and favor.

Honor the Lord with your entire heart. Those who "commit to [roll upon] the Lord " whatever they do, their "plans will succeed" (16:3). Wisdom is not offering a tit-for-tat arrangement for success with God in which a person can say, "Lord, I'm trusting in you, so bless me!" No, the Lord is not a heavenly Santa Claus who rewards someone for good behavior. Rather, the passage reflects a believer's life-style when he or she listens to wisdom and shares his or her entire life with the Lord. Such a person will know how God can establish his work. Wisdom desires to lead the believer whereby his faith "relieves much anxiety and smooths many perplexities."

An interesting promise to those who live godly is, "when man's ways are pleasing to the Lord, he makes even his enemies live at peace with him" (16:7). Even unbelievers will recognize the integrity of God's people and respect them. Not all unbelievers live in the gutter of life and drink the dregs of sin, even though they have not as yet come to faith. As already pointed out, man is created in the image of God, and because of common grace, he can appreciate righteousness and justice. Apart from God's fingerprints upon a man's soul, this world would indeed be a jungle. But the believer's life-style is a powerful appeal for unbelievers to respond to the Lord and come to faith.

The Lord takes delight in favoring His disciple. We have already seen how wisdom shouts loudly in the streets to all who will listen (1:20-21). Those who do give "heed to instruction" (lit., "act wisely") prosper, and there is special favor for the one "who trusts in the Lord" (16:20). In Old Testament days, when a person paid attention to the word wisdom wished to share, he or she knew how to trust in the Lord and experience genuine happiness and joy. Likewise, when people respond to Jesus, He offers not only eternal life but also shares with us the abundant life (John 10:10).

Another promise to the believer is that "the name of the Lord is a strong tower," and he or she can run to it in the midst of life's pressures and find safety (18:10). The name of the Lord is a truth rich in meaning; it relates to the holiness of His very being. Out of it come all His attributes, and His name is reflected in His righteousness, justice, omnipotence, omniscience, and a whole host of other comforting attributes. Many are the ideologies today in which men trust. But they do not afford any help for the long run in life. Hitler planned for his Third Reich, with its Nationalist Socialist ideology, to last for a thousand years. But after a mere twelve years in office, he died a meaningless death. The same can be said for materialism and secular humanism. All the goods of this world and all of the hopes for man's greatness apart from God can only end in dust and ashes. Those who trust in the Lord will enjoy His favor and never be ashamed.

As a believer trusts in the wisdom of God, he or she will find just the right mate. People may smile at the old saying "Marriages are made in heaven," but there is truth in the observation that, when God's purposes are served, He will provide a good wife as a "favor from the Lord" (18:22).

Sexual permissiveness, homosexuality, and lesbianism are signs that God's moral standards have been rejected. Earlier, wisdom's advice to the naive and inexperienced was to avoid the enticements of sexual freedom and involvement with the loose woman (2:16-19; 5:1-20; 6:24-29; 7:1-27). Righteous standards must be inculcated in the minds and hearts of children if society is to be redeemed from sure destruction.

But the negative stance should not be the only message. Conversely, parents need to speak positively about what it means to have a good family life and proper sexuality. Young people will generally respond to the wholesome love of a father and mother and adopt good moral standards as their own. "Houses and wealth are inherited from parents, but a prudent wife is from the Lord" (19:14). God is more interested in young people than they realize, and when they seek divine guidance, He delights to give each young man His gift of a good wife. Likewise, the Lord's good pleasure will give the godly young woman the husband of her dreams. But both parents and young people must realize that such gifts can only be realized when everyone understands they need to meet God's moral standards to enjoy the fullness of His favor.

Who can count the Lord's blessings? Proverbs 30 contains a list of enigmas, or hard to understand sayings (see Introduction). However, in one of the "sayings of Agur" (30:1), a special prayer in a group of four statements is addressed to the Lord (30:7-9). Agur's desire was to serve God acceptably, and so he pled with Him: "Two things I ask of you, O Lord; Do not refuse me before I die" (30:7). More than anything else, he wanted God's guidance all the days of his life. One petition in particular was his desire to rely on the wisdom of God so that falsehood and lies be kept far from him (30:8*a*). He was sensitive to the ninth commandment (Exodus 20:16), for he sought to avoid the sin of telling lies or testifying falsely against his neighbor. He only wanted the wisdom of God as his guide.

In his second request, Agur asked that the Lord should keep him from poverty. But, in addition, he wisely prayed that he should not have any more of this world's goods than he could handle (30:8*b*). He only wanted his "daily bread" (lit., "the bread of my portion"; 30:8*c*). This wisdom writer's underlying concern was that God should keep him far from covetousness as expressed in the tenth commandment. He wanted pure motives and priorities so that his life could be honorable to the Lord.

The New Testament equivalent is Paul's concern: "But godliness with contentment is great gain. For we brought nothing into the world, and we can take nothing out of it. But if we have food and clothing, we will be content with that. People who want to get rich fall into temptation and a trap" (1 Timothy 6:6-9). The writer to the Hebrews likewise reflected his concern to be kept from coveting: "Keep your lives free from the love of money and be content with what you have" (Hebrews 13:5).

Solomon took a lifetime to learn the difference between satisfying his *wants* and being content with moderation as to his *needs*. His considered advice, even for us today, is to "eat and drink and find satisfaction in . . . work" and "in . . . toilsome labor under the sun" (Ecclesiastes 2:24; 9:9). The Lord does not deprive comforts He designed for man, but neither does He want him to be so caught up in material things so as to forget his God. Rather, people must keep the Lord in the center of every pursuit of life. In particular, the believer must find his complete satisfaction in who God is and what He can provide.

The alternative is dreadful to contemplate. If life consists of more and more things, the danger is that a person can put God completely out of his life and even ask the question, "Who is the Lord?" (30:9*a*). The most disheartening attitude of the wealthy is forgetting that their wealth actually comes from the mercy and grace of God. The other depressing alternative is that the poor may steal a loaf of bread to keep body and soul together and thereby "dishonor the name of" their God (30:9*b-c*). What a beautiful prayer to the Lord by a person open to His guidance and wisdom. The Lord will have no difficulty blessing the life of anyone who is like-minded.

TRUST

The theme of trust appears eight times, and we have already seen its significance (3:5, 6; 3:26; 8:35). Trust is reflected in integrity whereby we can be completely open with our family and friends, as well as with the Lord. Unfortunately, the maintenance of trust can be fragile, and occasions arise when people find it extremely difficult to be completely honest. Parents can lie to their children, and they in turn do not share their hearts with the parents. Likewise, the main problem between a person and God is the sin nature that prevents trust in the Lord, who desires the best for each one's life. The book of Proverbs seeks to engage the interest of all people, the young in particular, that they may learn how to be open with the Lord and receive His wisdom for a lifetime of guidance.

The righteous (or believers) of the Old Testament had a promise they could implicitly trust: "The Lord does not let the righteous [lit., the soul of the righteous] go hungry" (10:3*a*). Mentioning the soul marks its extreme importance because in it is the seat of our desires and appetites. As long as they are legitimate and right, the Lord has promised the believer's basic needs for life. Likewise, "the blessing of the Lord brings wealth, and He adds no trouble to it" (10:22). We have already pointed out that Old Testament believers were promised that the Lord would provide abundantly in accordance with the Mosaic Constitution (see 3:9-10). Believers today, however, have a promise from God that He "will meet all" our needs (Philippians 4:19). Because we can trust God in what He has promised, whether Old or New Testaments, no anxiety or sadness need exist; rather, we can be content and at peace in our circumstances.

Another great promise is that "the way of the Lord is a refuge for the righteous" (10:29*a*). The Old Testament thought is that a person's "way" or "walk" refers to a life-style. When the Word of God is the guide for life-styles, believers can trust the Lord to be their refuge. Those who "do evil" will only find ruin and destruction.

The one who is good "obtains favor from the Lord" (12:2*a*). The term *good* is held out as an incentive to the young and inexperienced to choose a pious, godly life-style. He can then trust that the Lord will favor him. The "crafty man" (lit., "man of wicked devices"; 12:2*b*), however, can only look forward to condemnation and ruin. The father-teacher carefully outlines the life-style, but it is up to the individual to lay hold of and trust the Lord for the blessings only He can provide.

WISDOM

Passages teaching that the wisdom of the Lord is offered to all have been considered already (1:20-23; 2:6; 3:19; 8:22). If the young and inexperienced lay hold of practical wisdom, the Lord will enable them to live the best possible life-style. Through them God can then reach out to those who do not know Him. The apostle James offers the same possibility: "If any one of you lacks wis-

dom, he should ask God, who gives generously" (James
1:5). But James quickly adds a warning: "But when he
asks, he must believe and not doubt" (James 1:6). Believers today can offer our society a choice for great blessings.

RIGHTEOUSNESS

The moral standard God has given is nothing less
than His holiness, from which comes His righteousness.
Society today, however, assumes that morals are relative:
each person can do what is right in his own eyes. But God
cannot sanction such a belief and practice.

The marketplace. God's moral standards must in-
vade the marketplace, reminding men that "honest scales
and balances are from the Lord; all the weights in the bag
are of His making" (16:11). The Lord requires absolute
honesty and condemns everything that is false and unjust.
Captains in industry and those who are leaders in trading
centers are thereby warned that they will be held accountable if they manipulate the stock market and take advantage of situations where millions of dollars can be stolen.
God condemns evil practices that deprive associates or
poor people of their life's savings.

Vengeance. Righteousness is perverted when people
pay back wrongs perpetrated on them (20:22a). The only
godly response is to "wait for the Lord, and He will deliver
you" (20:22b). God's righteousness will save His followers
from the evil schemes of their enemies. They are not to
presume how He will judge but trust Him because He will
always judge in a righteous manner.

Our thoughts and motives. We live in a permissive
society. People choose the life-style that is most comfort-
able: "All of man's ways seem right to him" (21:2a; see
also 16:2a). The tragedy is that once a person has chosen
his own life-style for whatever purpose, he becomes smug
and content in his self-gratification. But the Lord knows
how to weigh the heart (21:2b) and the motives (16:2b).
The Spirit tests the deepest recesses of the heart, considering the reasons for their motives, priorities, and life-
styles. When people turn away from the Lord and His

standards, the Scripture warns: "Although they knew God, they neither glorified Him as God nor gave thanks to Him, but their *thinking became futile*" (Romans 1:21; italics added). We cannot escape His omniscience, and one day at the great white throne judgment, the Lord will judge unbelievers' motives and deeds as recorded in the books (Revelation 20:12).

The sayings of the wise men were that people should listen to God and take to heart His message. The wise teacher, therefore, emphasized "that your trust may be in the Lord, I teach you today, even you" (22:19). The young and inexperienced have knowledge from the Lord to live righteously in this present generation. God's way is not one of many possibilities; rather, the righteousness of God is good and pure, providing for the best possible life-style on this earth.

"Evil men do not understand justice" (28:5a) because they choose to ignore God's standards. The tragedy is that unrighteous people have minds that are bent or twisted in their understanding of God's right and good ways. They are not able to distinguish good from evil. They do not realize the consequences of their actions. But on the other hand, "those who seek the Lord understand it fully [lit., discriminate or distinguish all things]" (28:5b). "All things" refers to the righteous person who has an understanding of what is just for the affairs of life. The Lord has never left us without this information, and when anyone wishes to lay hold of God's standards of righteousness, they are always available.

The real authority. Many think that, if they can get the ear of some human authority, they will be able to twist his arm for special favors (29:26a). What people ought to realize is that leaders are only God's regents because "it is from the Lord that man gets justice" (29:26b). The human ruler has the responsibility to carry out God's standards, but should he flout them, he will not only demean and defile his position, he will also face certain judgment for his misdeeds.

Every person needs to understand that the Lord's righteousness cannot be ignored. Even though He does not choose to answer and judge evil people any day of the week, His day of reckoning will come soon enough for those who turn away from His righteousness.

CURSE, WICKEDNESS

Four times the book of Proverbs mentions the fearful actions of God's curse, and one of these has already been considered in 3:33.

Prayer is a part of the Lord's plan, and He takes great delight when "He hears the prayer of the righteous" (15:29*b*). The wicked, however, are far from the Lord, and although He certainly hears their prayers, He is under no constraint to answer them. The thoughts of the wicked are perverted by sin, and even though they may pray, the Lord has distanced Himself from them because He cannot fellowship with their evil deeds.

Wisdom, unfortunately, has to comment on how "a man's own folly ruins his life" (lit., "the foolishness of man perverts his way"; 19:3*a*). When a man, woman, or young person persists in the foolishness of rejecting the Lord's wisdom, such decisions will only lead to ruin in the long run. In the upside-down way of the world's thinking, evil people never take the blame for their wrong decisions. Instead they rail against God: "Yet his heart rages against the Lord" (19:3*b*). Man's failures, however, are the result of his own stubbornness, and, in particular, the young and inexperienced need to be prepared for life by having God's standards drilled into their hearts and minds. We must never attribute to God the results of our own choices contrary to His righteousness.

Genesis offers an illustration of how fearful it becomes when people are apprehended for their wicked deeds, even though committed many years before. Joseph's brothers came to Egypt to buy grain for themselves, their father, and others in Canaan (Genesis 42:1-24). After being accused of being spies, held in prison for three days, and then asked to leave one of their clan behind in Egypt so as to return to Canaan and bring Benjamin on their next visit, they exclaimed, "Surely we are being punished because of our brother" (42:21). Reuben added, "Didn't I tell you not to sin against the boy?" (42:22). When God in His providence brought the brothers face to face with Joseph (although they had not as yet recognized him), they were conscious-stricken for the way they had treated Joseph and for their lies to Jacob (Genesis 37:32-33). Likewise, when unregenerate people face the Lord at the great white throne judgment, their own deeds will rise up to testify against them (Revelation 20:12-13). At that time, they will not be able to point the finger at someone else or blame God for any of their misfortune.

A final example of wickedness points again to one of the main themes of Proverbs: "The mouth of an adulteress is a deep pit" (22:14a). The young and inexperienced have already been warned of her smooth and seductive speech (see 2:16; 7:21). Far from being attractive, however, her smooth words are actually a deep pit, similar to what hunters set for animals (see 23:27). Should the young and inexperienced not take to heart this particular standard set by wisdom, the person "who is under the Lord's wrath will fall into it" (22:14b). Literally, such a person is detested by the Lord, and He will show no mercy to the unregenerate and reprobate who insist that sexual permissiveness is an option for a valid life-style.

NO VINDICTIVENESS

People generally delight in having their own way. Wisdom warns, however, to "not [even begin to] gloat when your enemy falls; when he stumbles, do not let your heart [even begin to] rejoice" (24:17). The admonition strikes at inner attitudes that would take satisfaction with someone else's misfortune.

Israel had every reason to gloat over the fall of the Egyptians. They lost their first-born. Then the flower of their army perished when the Red Sea closed over them. Yet, at the Passover, the second of four cups of wine is designated as the Cup of the Plagues. Before partaking, the leader empties the cup of ten drops, one drop for each plague. Everyone is thereby reminded that their joy must be lessened so as to not take satisfaction over those who had once been their severe taskmasters.

If this warning is not heeded, the Lord will not overlook such vindictiveness and will "disapprove and turn His wrath away from him" (24:18). He may actually turn away His judgment from the enemy He hates and take action against the one who has revenge in his heart. While the archangel Michael had every reason to curse Satan, the enemy of God, nevertheless he "did not dare to bring a slanderous accusation against him, but said, 'The Lord rebuke you!'" (Jude 9). There is no doubt that we live in a world where the ungodly delight in slander, accusation, and revenge-taking, but such ungodly behavior is only a reflection of how Satan operates. He is the master of vindictiveness.

DISCIPLINE, CARE FOR THE POOR,
AND CARE FOR THE ENEMY

Care for the poor. This is a most important matter in the Mosaic Constitution and is echoed in Proverbs. While the natural tendency by those who have means is to look down on and even ignore the poor, God holds the believer responsible for having compassion on the disadvantaged. Wisdom reminds us, "He who is kind to the poor lends to the Lord, and He will reward him for what he has done" (19:17). The word for "what he has done" actually refers to a benefit, as, for example, the Lord's benefits (Psalm 103:2a). The point of wisdom's lesson is that when a person lends to the Lord, he becomes God's creditor, and there can be no safer investment because He is the refuge for the poor (Psalm 14:6).

Are the poor person and the oppressor any different? The two stand as equals before God: "The poor man and the oppressor have this in common: the Lord gives sight to the eyes of both" (29:13). He not only wants them to realize that He gives life to both of them, the oppressor is strongly reminded to regard the poor with compassion because both came from the same clay, and, together, they will return to dust. Therefore, the one with means is reminded that he is his brother's keeper.

The Mosaic Covenant had a number of ways by which the poor could be cared for:

1. They could glean in the fields after the harvest or pick up grapes that had fallen to the ground in the vineyard (Leviticus 19:9-10).
2. A poor farmer could sell the crop value of his land until the following year of Jubilee. Land itself was never to be sold, but a fair price could be given to the farmer "on the basis of the number of years left for harvesting crops" (Leviticus 25:15). At the following year of Jubilee (if the land had not been redeemed), the use of the land reverted back to the original land owner.
3. He could borrow money from those with means at no interest. It was simply a case where the wealthy must help the poor. Charging interest was stealing, and when the rich tried to take it, he would only make himself obnoxious by trying to make a profit on a person's misery (Deuteronomy 23:19-20).
4. Every third and sixth year of the Sabbatical cycle, the fellowship tithe was to be given to the poor, possibly during the feast of Tabernacles (Deuteronomy 26:12-15).
5. If the situation became desperate, a poor person could hire himself out to a well-to-do Israeli. The poor man was to serve for six years, but on the seventh he was set free and amply supplied with food and seed. The man who was once poor could now have a fresh start (Deuteronomy 15:12-15).

The Mosaic Constitution is one of the best documents detailing the means of taking care of the poor. The law never gave instruction on how to do away with the poverty cycle, but it did reveal how God wanted those with means to have compassion on those less fortunate.

Care for the enemy. Wisdom's instruction for the care of an enemy runs counter to this world's standards. The unregenerate frequently deliberately take vengeance on those they dislike, thereby doing them great harm. But

God has a better way: "If your enemy is hungry, give him food to eat; if he is thirsty, give him water to drink" (25:21). Wisdom encourages believers to look for ways and means of helping their enemies, as much as possible. When they do, their good deeds will be as "burning coals on" the heads of their enemies "and the Lord will reward" them (25:22). After all, "He causes His sun to rise on the evil and the good, and sends rain on the righteous and the unrighteous" (Matthew 5:45). Paul echoes the same sentiments: "If your enemy is hungry, feed him; if he is thirsty, give him something to drink. In doing this, you will heap burning coals on his head" (Romans 12:20). By returning good for evil, the believer follows the divine plan to make the unregenerate sorry for acting so despicably. The Lord will care for His own who choose to act as God does.

Child care. Finally, wisdom provides a word concerning the parents' care for children (29:15), but we shall discuss this further in chapter 10 when dealing with the correction of children and adolescents.

GOD AND MAN

Most of the passages in Proverbs relate man to the covenant name LORD, but other names for God are used as well, and we shall examine them now in more detail.

ELOHA/ELOHIM

The general name for God in Semitic languages across the Middle East is *El*, and this word appears in the Hebrew Old Testament, in Aramaic, Arabic, and in other languages. Another word is *Eloha*, which is the singular name for God, the plural being *Elohim*. *Eloha* is not widely used, but when it appears, it is usually in a poetic context. It appears elsewhere only in the book of Job, where both saint and unbeliever appropriate this general name, each from his own frame of reference.

The one time *Eloha* appears in the book of Proverbs it underscores the Word of God as the only correct guide to follow: "Every word of God [*Eloha*] is flawless; He is a shield to those who take refuge in Him" (30:5). We will never fully grasp the essence of God or have *all* knowledge. However, God does reveal to us practical knowledge, which is within everyone's reach. When we take refuge in His word, He shields us from the enemy of our souls. Paul no doubt drew from this verse when he said, "take up the shield of faith, with which you can extinguish all the flaming arrows of the evil one" (Ephesians 6:16). Our faith in God's revelation, with its practical knowledge, is what will enable us to be overcomers.

Elohim appears five times in Proverbs. It is the most commonly used general name for God in thè Old Testament, primarily expressing the limitless expanse of the majesty of God. His greatness and majesty suggest that God is able to do for us beyond what we can ask or think because of His limitless power or omnipotence. This particular name is associated with creation, since it appears already in the first verse of the Bible, "In the beginning God [*Elohim*] created the heavens and the earth" (Genesis 1:1).

Three of its uses have already been considered: finding the "knowledge of God" (2:5); the adulterer ignoring "the covenant she made before God" (2:17); and the believer having favor and a good name in the sight of God and man (3:4).

In a strange statement, wisdom declares, "It is the glory of God to conceal a matter" (25:2a). This sometimes makes it difficult to ascertain the purposes of God's will. (See Deuteronomy 29:29 and Isaiah 45:15 for similar situations.) During these times, especially when in deep waters and sorrow, we may feel that God has deserted us. Obviously, He has not, but these are occasions of testing that we may grow in faith. At other times, He can and does willingly share His will with us freely. It is the "glory of kings . . . to search out a matter" (25:2b). As the regents of God their investigation and measured pronouncement may share a wisdom everyone can accept.

HOLY ONE

Twice this peculiar designation for God appears in the book of Proverbs, marking the very essence of God as holy. The first is in 9:10 where, at the invitation of wisdom as a gracious host, the young and inexperienced can grasp that the "knowledge of the Holy One is understanding." This emphasis is repeated in the sayings of Agur, who admitted his deficiency as he cried out for the possibility to learn "wisdom" and have the "knowledge of the Holy One" (30:3). When anyone takes a humble position before the Lord, admitting his or her lack of skill, knowledge, and understanding, God is more than willing to reveal Himself. He reminds us that His Word is flawless and that it is a shield for those who take refuge in Him (30:5). People can never say that they are without moral guidelines. They can either be blessed by them or condemned by them.

He who gets wisdom loves his own soul;
he who cherishes understanding propers.

Proverbs 19:8

A man who lacks judgment derides his neighbor,
but a man of understanding holds his tongue.

Proverbs 11:12

9

THE BELIEVER AND HIS EMOTIONS

In this chapter we discover what the book of Proverbs has to say regarding emotions and how to achieve a balance in the emotional life. Emotions can be expressed through anger, joy, grief, love, and fear. Generally there are two groups of emotions. Frustration results when a person is prevented from doing what he would like to do, which may lead to emotions of anger, hate, or even fear. These are disagreeable emotions, and the book of Proverbs names a number of them by which a person can become insecure. The desirable emotions, such as love and joy, make it possible for a person to be well-adjusted and able to achieve the highest goals in life.

EMOTIONAL BEINGS

A definite link exists between emotions and the outward, physical countenance. When a person is joyful, he expresses it through laughter or a smile. On the other hand, a clenched fist or a jaw clamped shut betrays anger. The emotion of grief is expressed in tears and sobs. A fearful person displays symptoms of tenseness.

Emotions, however, can also exert a far more serious toll on the body. A link also exists between emotions and inner changes in the physical system. Anger, rage, and fear, to mention a few, can cause the heart to beat faster, the face to flush, breathing rate to increase, and blood pressure to rise. A person's blood supply goes to the muscles, and the adrenal glands pour their secretions into the blood stream. If the emotions last longer than a few moments, the thyroid gland speeds up its secretions and the digestive system can slow down and even stop.

High emotional levels can harm the body. A state of continual anxiety or worry upsets the digestive system, and stomach ulcers can develop (although not all ulcer conditions are due to emotional highs). When the body chemistry is altered sufficiently, a person suffers physically.

The book of Proverbs does not attempt to develop a highly complicated system of psychology to deal with all the emotional needs of a man or woman. In a practical way, however, this book names both pleasurable and undesirable emotions, then proceeds to encourage a person to pursue those that are agreeable. To become involved with disagreeable emotions is to harm body, soul, and spirit.

The Holy Spirit, who regenerates the unbeliever, also provides the means of expressing pleasurable emotions in a well-adjusted emotional life. Many times emotional stability attracts unbelievers to Christ, creating a hunger in their hearts for spiritual things.

PLEASURABLE EMOTIONS

JOY

Joy is the peculiar possession of those who make a practice of counseling peace or who act in the role of peacemakers. There is "joy for those who promote peace" (12:20). Jesus identified peacemaking as one of the great beatitudes and said such a person is filled with genuine happiness, actually joy (Matthew 5:9).

In a perverted sense, those who find joy in committing folly are said to lack "judgment" (lit., "lack heart"; 15:21). Such a person walks a crooked course. A man of true "understanding" does not find joy in folly. Instead, he "keeps a straight course" (15:21*b*). The "righteous one," an Old Testament designation for the believer, *acts* righteously and with "justice." Such a person is filled with joy (21:15*a*). This experience of joy reflects biblical standards and principles. Only the one born anew and living a life that demonstrates the new dynamic will have genuine joy.

Speech and *words* (see chapter 11) also interconnect with the emotion of joy. Wisdom declares that "a man finds joy in giving an apt reply—and how good is a timely word" (15:23). Such words will have a most beneficial effect upon society.

Joy is very much intertwined in one's relationship with parents (see chapter 10). A child who heeds the wise instruction of his parents and teachers brings joy to his parents: "The father of a righteous man has great joy; he who has a wise son delights in him" (23:24). How important for parents to provide opportunities for their children to acquire wisdom. On the other hand, "There is no joy for the father of a fool" (17:21*b*). Parents are in anguish when their child goes astray, either because of stubbornness or because the parents have somehow failed as role models.

Emotions stem from a person's innermost feelings: "Each heart knows its own bitterness, and no one else can share its joy" (14:10). Difficult indeed is it to make another understand a time of bitter sorrow or great joy. This verse does not mean that sorrows or joys cannot be shared with others, though the former is the more difficult of the two. Rather, innermost feelings cannot be fully shared as they have been privately experienced.

CHEERFULNESS, MERRIMENT

These words are quite interesting. Cheerfulness is basically the idea of "goodness" or "gladness." The emotion represented by "merriment" expresses happiness or rejoicing. The "happy [or, merry, rejoicing] heart makes the face cheerful [lit., good]" (15:13*a*). The expression of the heart makes itself visible in the face, and the "cheerful [good] heart has a continual feast" (15:15b). How true. What a man thinks within himself, so is he. In a negative sense, "do not eat the food of a stingy man . . . for he is the kind of man who is always thinking about the cost. 'Eat and drink,' he says to you, but his heart is not with you" (23:6-7). What is in his heart is no doubt visible on his dour face. Likewise, the one who has a happy heart has a cheerful face.

This connection of heart and face also affects health. "A cheerful [rejoicing] heart is good medicine" (lit., "the joyful heart causes a good healing"; 17:22). When God rejoices the heart, the whole body benefits, and such a person is calm in his spirit. No wonder the face reveals volumes as to one's physical, emotional, and spiritual condition. But the real source of cheerfulness is trust "in the Lord" (16:20).

PRAISE

The psalmist declared, "It is fitting for the upright to praise him" (Psalm 33:1b). Only believers, the righteous ones, are able to speak in this way from the heart. What a sheer delight to be in the presence of one who can praise the Lord from the heart.

Wisdom reminds us that our conduct and testimony as believers should be of such quality that even unbelievers respond with words of praise. Sometimes we are tested through various kinds of situations, and God permits these circumstances to reveal our character: "The crucible [is] for silver and the furnace [is] for gold, but man is tested by the praise he receives" (27:21). We are judged many times by people around us and need, therefore, to guard carefully our testimony, even in those times when life's circumstances are difficult. Wisdom's further comment is the reminder to "let another praise you, and not your own mouth; someone else, and not your own lips" (27:2).

This phenomenon of assessing character is also applied to the diligent wife who "watches over the affairs of her household" (31:27a). The careful, honest, and wise wife is praised by her husband for her "noble character" and labor of love (31:28b). She is even known at the gates of the city (actually the meeting place of the elders in a kind of city council), where "her works bring her praise" (31:31b). This is "the woman who fears the Lord," and because she has a special relationship to Him, she "is to be praised" (31:30b).

God honors the man who walks with the Lord in the midst of life's trials. Similarly, He respects the woman who is a godly wife and mother, who speaks "with wisdom" and whose lips are a glory and praise to Him (31:26). On the other hand, those who "praise the wicked" only reflect their perverted, twisted sense of values because they have forsaken "the law" (or, divine instruction; 28:4).

DELIGHT

Delight is an emotion that produces a multiplicity of feelings. One such shade of meaning expresses beauty and pleasantness: "It will go well with [lit., will be a delight to] those who convict the guilty" (24:25a). The text may sound strange because most of us do not find it pleasant to rebuke anyone. But no spirit of maliciousness is implied. Rather, the parent or teacher, under God's direction, has to take this course of action at times for the character training of his charges. The goal is to help them make the right choices in life, to avoid wrongdoing and choose what is right. "Rich blessing will come upon" those involved in such forthright training (24:25b).

Another shade of meaning refers to what is delicious as food but which also gives extreme pleasure to the soul. When parents have to "discipline" their sons and daughters, they will have a reward someday when their offspring are right morally and spiritually. The feeling of a child-training task done well will give peace and bring delight to the soul (29:17).

Five occurrences of *delight* reflect goodwill and acceptance:

146 Savoring the Wisdom of Proverbs

1. The business merchant who is a believer and uses "accurate weights" on the scales is accepted by God (11:1*b*).
2. "Those whose ways are blameless," that is, those who live righteously are also accepted by God (11:20*b*).
3. The Lord "delights in men who are" in the habit of *acting* truthfully (lit., faithfully), as well as speaking truthfully (12:22*b*).
4. "The prayer of the upright pleases him" (15:8*b*). Not only should a person be accepted by God, but he should also be accepted by his peers and authorities.
5. The "man who speaks the truth" is valued by kings (16:13).

By contrast, in a perverted sense of delight, is the fool who "finds no pleasure [or, takes no delight] in understanding [or, distinguishing between good and evil]" (18:2*a*).

GLADNESS OR JOY

This emotion describes our divinely given capacity to be glad in the soul. Of the eight times this word appears in Proverbs, four picture the relationship between parents and their children. The son who is wise because he has obeyed his parents' godly instruction "brings joy to his father" (10:1*a*; 15:20*a*). Wise and righteous sons and daughters give their parents every good reason to "be glad" or merry (23:25*a*). How much better are they than rebellious offspring who only give grief to their parents' hearts. Children are, therefore, encouraged to be wise and "bring joy" to the hearts of parents and teachers (27:11*a*).

Other appearances of this word in a variety of contexts are interesting. "An anxious heart weighs a man down, but a kind word cheers him [or, makes him glad]" (12:25). Encouragement is a precious commodity in society. "The prospect" for hope by "the righteous is joy" (10:28*a*). On the other hand, "the hopes of the wicked come to nothing" (10:28*b*). The believer particularly has a joyful disposition because he has already settled his relationship with the Lord, and that hope impacts everyday living for the here and now.

One use of the word *glad* conveys the idea of inward excitement, yet we should never "rejoice" (be excited to gladness) when an "enemy . . . stumbles" (24:17). For "the Lord will see and disapprove and turn his wrath away from him" (24:18). In particular, the believer is never to take revenge on his enemy; the Lord Himself declares that "it is mine to avenge; I will repay. In due time their foot will slip" (Deuteronomy 32:35). Another passage contains the warning that "whoever gloats [or, is glad] over disaster will not go unpunished" (17:5*b*). Why should any believer laugh at someone else's calamity and misfortune?

REJOICING

The specific emotion of rejoicing also reflects several shades of meaning in the book of Proverbs. Of fourteen occurrences of "rejoice," eight reflect the idea of a joyous experience—exulting, obtaining pleasure from, being glad. They are enumerated as follows:

1. "The light of the righteous shines brightly [lit., rejoices]" (13:9*a*) perhaps indicates that the ever-shining light of God within a believer burns joyfully.

2. "A cheerful look [lit., the light of the eyes] brings joy to the heart" (15:30*a*). Pleasant sensations to the eye or ear can rejoice the heart and remove sadness from it. Paul's encouragement in the book of Philippians is helpful when he suggests that the believer ponder what is "true . . . pure . . . lovely"; these are the elements that enable believers to have hearts of rejoicing (Philippians 4:8).

3. The parent appeals to his son, the teacher to his charge, saying, "My son, if your heart is wise. . . ." The implication of the appeal is that the young person should gladly accept the guideline to "speak what is right" (23:16*b*) and do what is godly. If he responds correctly, then the heart of the parent or teacher "will be glad" (23:15*b*).

4. We are reminded that we should "not gloat [or, rejoice]" inwardly when our enemies fall (24:17).
5. One puzzling statement requires some extra research to understand its meaning: "Perfume and incense bring joy to the heart" (27:9a). On a number of occasions, the Old Testament describes women who use fragrant ointment ("oil of myrrh . . . perfumes and cosmetics"; Esther 2:12) or cosmetic perfume ("myrrh and incense"; Song of Solomon 3:6). Tastefully used, cosmetics can enhance a woman's beauty, and through the aesthetics of sight and smell, a man's deepest passions are aroused. Wisdom, however, makes good use of such aesthetics to teach in the parallel of the passage that the "pleasantness [lit., sweetness] of one's friend springs from his earnest counsel [lit., the counsel of the soul]" (27:9b). God can take what man perverts and turn it around to teach a profound and precious lesson.
6. "When the righteous thrive," that is, when good men attain authority in the political process, all "the people rejoice" (29:2a). As the people of God pray, godly men rule well in the highest levels of government. By contrast, this is antithetically paralleled by "when the wicked rule," they become tyrants and "the people groan" (29:2b).
7. "A man [or woman] who loves wisdom brings joy to his [or her] father" (29:3a). What indeed can be more gratifying to a father?
8. The believer of the Old Testament "can sing and be glad [or, rejoice]" (29:6b). Believers today can do the same. Though pleasure can be enjoyed for a short time (Hebrews 11:25), God's people enjoy genuine blessings.

Another connotation of *rejoice* is to become excited: "The father of a righteous man has great joy" or real inward excitement (23:24a). The mother whose children live for the Lord can also rejoice with strong inner feelings (23:25b).

To exult is another shade of meaning: an entire "city rejoices [or, exults]" (11:10a); and "when the righteous triumph [or, exult], there is great elation" (28:12a). In the latter instance, the assumption is that the righteous will make good use of their prosperity. While the general public might not like what a believer stands for, the antithetic parallel teaches that, in the majority of instances when believers are in office, they wisely use the resources of the people for great blessing.

Another aspect of rejoicing is *being jubilant*: "my inmost being will rejoice" when the lips of sons and daughters "speak what is right" (23:16). The "inmost being" can refer to the kidneys, suggesting again the direct connection between emotions and various parts of the body. Pleasant emotions contribute to good health, but tragically the opposite is also true.

One curious concept of *rejoice* is to *laugh* or *jest*. The model wife, because of her sense of strength, dignity, and wise management, can "laugh at the days to come" (31:25b). She does not have to worry. She has prepared for every eventuality for her family and herself and, therefore, has a sense of confidence as she faces the future.

LOVE

Without doubt, love stands high on the list of pleasurable emotions. This deepest and most meaningful of all emotions is the glue that holds family and friends together. The love of God gives meaning to life, and the love we have for God comes out of the deepest feelings of gratitude and esteem we have for His love toward us.

Proverbs 7-8 emphasizes love for wisdom (8:17), seeking wisdom early (8:17), and even the perverted sense of love (7:18). Although this word abounds in the Old Testament, it appears in the book of Proverbs only nineteen times. Eighteen times it describes human relationships and once conveys the idea of what is good. There are no appearances of the word in its deepest covenantal sense —the loving-kindness of God; instead, Proverbs focuses primarily on practical, everyday affairs of life.

The love for wisdom and instruction, and what this emotion can do for human relationships, is paramount; eight of the previously mentioned eighteen verses are given to this emphasis. The one "who loves discipline [or, instruction] loves knowledge" (12:1*a*). Such a person seeks instruction so that he can have the best possible means for living a godly life. In a special way God "loves those who pursue righteousness" (15:9*b*). He can trust them to represent Him among the world of men. The man and woman "who speaks the truth" are valued (lit., loved; 16:13*b*). Although liars and cheaters hate those who speak the truth, yet truth-telling in general is highly respected. The person "who covers over an offense," that is, turns away from or forgets a wrong done to him, "promotes love, but whoever repeats the matter separates close friends" (17:9). Many of the people of this world act contrary to such behavior, but if one is tolerant and turns the other cheek, a friendship eventually can be forged with such ungodly folk for the cause of the gospel.

The person who seeks wisdom acquires a heart of understanding (see 7:7 and 9:4, where judgment is lit. *heart*). Likewise, the one "who gets wisdom loves his own soul" (19:8*a*). People who diligently lay hold of God's wisdom will be rewarded by finding what is valuable in life. Even the king is the friend of a person "who loves a pure heart and whose speech is gracious" (22:11). Civil authorities find that people who have these qualities rest easier in their jobs. The believer in this sense is assuredly salt for society.

The wisdom writer also reminds us that "open rebuke" is better than "hidden love" (27:5). The greatest love of all is when, with sensitivity, a person is open and candid with those who need correction and guidance. The believer who remains silent because of a "love" that wishes to spare a person's feelings is not forthright. In fact, this is not acting in a loving way at all.

Once again, Proverbs emphasizes what is most important for parents and their offspring. The person "who loves wisdom brings joy to his father" (29:3). As parents age, nothing brings more delight to them than to see the achievements of their offspring. But the greatest satisfaction of all is to see children mature in the Lord, serving Him with their whole hearts.

Love can also be perverted, and there is no greater tragedy than to see it misused. Proverbs warns against this kind of love five times:

1. When one "resents correction," he is called a mocker (15:12*a*). Loving reproof is intended by wisdom to give a person values for life, but all too often it is refused. This refusal is vividly seen in families with rebellious children and by employees who do sloppy work. As a result, society cannot attain the excellence God desires.
2. Anyone who "loves a quarrel" is a pervert because he "loves sin [lit., strife]" (17:19*a*).
3. The person who loves his or her foul use of the tongue will certainly "eat its fruit" (18:21). The ungodly know how to curse, tell shady stories, lie, and blaspheme, but the end result of such conversation only finds the offender on the way to death.
4. The one "who loves pleasure" for its own sake, squandering it on him or herself, "will become poor" (21:17*a*).
5. How can anyone be responsible when he "loves wine" in a constant round of banquets and the continual anointing of the body with "oil," testing out all the latest smells of perfume. No wonder such people have no money when the time of need comes (21:17*b*).

The role of love in the desire for peacemaking is again emphasized. "Love covers all wrongs" (10:12*b*), that is, makes invisible even gross sins. Peter seems to refer to this proverb when he says, "Love covers over a multitude of sins" (1 Peter 4:8). Evidently this phrase was a popular saying at the time. Paul also alluded to the same idea in his famous love chapter when from his heart he yearned to see a love that "always protects [or, covers]" and "always perseveres" (1 Corinthians 13:7). The one who is filled with the love of God can quiet the troubled waters in a family or community and yet not overlook evil. In another dimension wisdom observes that "better [is] a meal of vegetables where there is love than a fattened calf with hatred" (15:17). The food goes down better when one can enjoy it without anxiety.

The lazy person is warned not to "love sleep" because in the end he "will grow poor" and have nothing with which to pay his bills (20:13a). Parents are encouraged to discipline their children when it is needed to demonstrate that they really care for and love them (13:24). (We shall come back to this discussion in chapter 10.)

In a curious single occurrence is found, "To be esteemed [or, favored, lovingly favored] is better than silver or gold" (22:1b). Literally, the "good favor" is best (even though this is an awkward phrase). But to understand why, we need the full perspective of the lesson in this passage:

> A good name is more desirable than great riches;
> to be esteemed is better than silver or gold (22:1).

A person's name parallels what is esteemed or what is considered to be "good favor": a name or reputation held in favor by all people is more desirable than the great treasure of the world.

TRANQUILLITY

Many today seek "peace of mind" and calm spirits, but no amount of tranquilizers, transcendental meditation, or yoga can provide tranquillity for today's restless generation. One of the reasons for emotional instability stems from what people miss in a personal relationship with the Lord.

One way to enjoy tranquillity is to realize the fulfillment of genuine desires: "Hope deferred makes the heart sick, but a longing fulfilled is a tree of life" (13:12). But if what we hope for is dragged out day after day and even year after year, the heart becomes sick and the body can even suffer pain. Unbelievers know this too well when they pin their hopes on what can be gained in this world only to be disappointed. However, when moral and godly desires are fulfilled, their fruition is as a tree of life, an expression that depicts, in one sense, the enjoyment of happiness in the soul.

Consider also how "a longing fulfilled is sweet to the soul" (13:19a). The wife who waits for her husband to come home from war, the mother who waits for her hostage son to return, the parents who wait expectantly for their children to receive Christ, these and a whole host of desires fulfilled are the experiences into which we all enter. When they are fulfilled, we can rejoice and enjoy great happiness.

The analogy of having sufficient food reflects tranquillity of soul: "The righteous eat to their hearts' content [lit., the satisfaction of their soul, or desire]" (13:25a). He eats only as much as will satisfy him, "but the stomach of the wicked grows hungry" (13:25b). The latter lack inner peace and never seem to have enough. The one who seeks to please God knows that his life does not consist in mere intake of food, but the restless unbeliever only eats and eats, trying to compensate for what he or she does not have.

Proper speech also promotes tranquillity: "From the fruit of his lips a man is filled [or, satisfied] with good things" (12:14a). In chapter 11, we shall discuss further the importance of right speech, but even now we see that those who speak wise words of encouragement and comfort to people in need will find a sense of satisfaction and tranquillity for themselves. What goes forth in both speech and deeds will return with blessing to the sender.

PITY

The meaning of *pity* conveys the idea of being gracious to those who do not have this world's goods: "He who is kind [or, gracious] to the poor lends to the Lord, and he will reward him for what he had done" (19:17). In a similar curious occurrence of being gracious (showing pity), "he who increases his wealth by exorbitant interest" (28:8a) to fatten his own bank account—illegal in the Old Testament (Leviticus 25:36)—"amasses it for another, who will be kind to the poor" (28:8). Ill-gotten wealth will in some way revert to the righteous, who may then use it to help the poor. Right eventually does prevail because the

Lord has a way of evening out the accounts. Wisdom teaches us, however, to show a sense of graciousness (pity) to those in need.

UNDESIRABLE EMOTIONS

The book of Proverbs refers to a broad cross section of emotions, including some disagreeable and unhappy ones. Often these undesirable emotions reflect wrong choices and evil deeds that result because of man's fallen nature. But simply being in unpleasant surroundings can also make people disagreeable.

Sometimes undesirable emotions are not at all wrong. When confronted by danger, for example, a person properly registers fear, and the body compensates through extra adrenaline to give him or her the extra strength necessary to avert disaster. Nevertheless, the list of undesirable emotions in Proverbs provides helpful insight into our human natures.

SCORN

Scorn for parents, neighbors, civil authorities, or even God only demonstrates the evil in a person's heart. Seven occurrences of this term reflect various shades of meaning. "He who scorns instruction [lit., the entire Word of God] will pay for it" (13:13a). A person cannot turn his back on the spiritual and moral message of the Word without being held accountable to the Lord Himself. Neither should he "speak to a fool," that is, give him advice or instruction (23:9a). The latter will only "scorn the wisdom of [his] words" (23:9b), and his words will be wasted.

The one who "derides his neighbor," possibly even in public denunciation, only reveals that he "lacks judgment" (lit., lacks heart or sense; 11:12a). In addition, "he who despises his neighbor sins" (14:21a). Because the second line encourages a person to "be kind to the needy" (14:21b), we can assume that the sin referred to in the first line is to ignore or drive away the one who is afflicted or poor. God observes how we treat our neighbor. Those who have such "warped minds [lit., hearts]" that they scorn wisdom will be "despised" by her in return (12:8b). Possibly one of the worst cases of a bad attitude and evil heart is when offspring scorn their parents. Sons and daughters are warned not even to begin to "despise [their] mother when she is old" (23:22b). Too frequently the oft-repeated adage is true: a mother can care for ten children; but when she is old and can no longer care for herself, these same ten cannot take care of one mother. Worse yet, they may trundle her off to a nursing home for the least reason. Obviously, there are times when a mother needs extra care, but she should not be despised when she is helpless. The writer adds that "the eye that mocks a father, that scorns obedience to a mother, will be pecked out by the ravens of the valley, will be eaten by the vultures" (30:17). What a bitter price to pay for the evil of scorn. (We shall discuss further the subject of parents and home in chapter 10.)

Another word picture describes the one who raises his head loftily and disdains both people and God. The person "whose ways are devious despises" the Lord (14:2b). The one who "despises his mother" is called a "foolish man" (15:20b), while the person who disobeys "instructions" regarding "his soul" and becomes "contemptuous of [despises] his ways will die" (19:16b). The latter statement describes the man or woman who does not have regard for godly conduct, and God will judge them both with the punishment of death.

The book of Proverbs contains three more pictures of contempt or scorn. The first is *to loathe.* The person who "ignores [or, refuses] discipline despises [that is, loathes] himself" (15:32a). He really has little concern for who he is or what he does, possibly because he has such a low self-image. The second picture is the idea of *contempt* or spurning. The one who "spurns his father's discipline" is "a fool" (15:5a). The third is, literally, *to slight* or show no esteem, which needs some explanation. "Better to be a nobody [or, lightly esteemed] and yet have a servant than pretend to be somebody [or, honor himself] and have no food" (12:9). Wisdom is not suggesting that we should prize a low self-esteem; rather, the comparison is offered so that the person who is in modest circumstances is much better off than the one who "plays the man of rank," when in reality he lacks even the bare necessities of life.

In many ways wisdom gives us ample warning to avoid or squelch this reprehensible emotion. When we demean others we actually demean man's dignity. But man only has dignity because he bears God's image. So, when man is insulted by his fellow man, God Himself is demeaned. We need to watch, therefore, how we talk to one another.

ANGER, WRATH

Though anger is deplorable, especially if unjustified, there are times when circumstances warrant righteous indignation. Even Jesus displayed anger at people when they were apathetic with or callous toward the things of God. Proverbs contains six different shades of meaning for words translated "anger" or "wrath."

The shade of meaning used most often is literally translated "nose" ('*af*) and is used figuratively of anger, either because anger usually reddens the face, particularly the nose, or because anger causes the nose to dilate and breathing to become more intense. Many times an angry person does not even have to say a word for everyone around to sense the anger. This word is used ten times, but we will examine only a few of them.

"A patient man [or, he who is slow to anger] has great understanding [or, discriminatory judgment]" (14:29a). This is the person who has learned to control his anger. Wisdom repeats the advice: "The patient man" can pacify the "hot-tempered man [who] stirs up dissension" (15:18). After all, it takes two to fight, but if one is not so disposed, he has it in his power to control undesirable anger. Again, "better a patient man than a warrior" (16:32a) ready for a fight.

How can we control our anger? Wisdom offers some clues. "A man's wisdom [prudence or good sense] gives him patience [or, makes him slow to anger] (19:11*a*), and "a gift given in secret soothes anger" (21:14*a*). Wisdom does not condone bribery, but there are times when the believer's common sense can prevail to pacify unbelievers.

A Christian was once set upon by an angry woman who rebuked her in public. On the woman's next birthday the Christian gave her tormenter a gift, and ever afterward the two women have been the best of friends. Wisdom adds, "Wise men turn away anger" (29:8*b*), and in fact the peacemaker is the one who has learned how to apply God's directives in situations that could otherwise become explosive.

An interesting word picture of anger relates to a scene down on the farm: "As churning the milk produces butter, and as twisting the nose [perhaps, blowing it with force] produces blood," so it will not be long before "stirring up anger produces strife" (30:33). The rising pitch of angry words will soon lead to a full-scale fight.

The second shade of meaning used most for anger often describes *burning anger* or the heat that comes with uncontrolled anger. The word *hamah* (to be hot) has greater force and stronger meaning than *'af*. *Hamah* appears six times in the book of Proverbs.

The "hot-tempered man stirs up dissension" (15:18*a*). It's best to stay out of his way. An even worse situation is when a king or a civil authority is possessed by "wrath," for it can bring "death" to his subjects (16:14*a*). Yet the "wise man," perhaps a trusted friend or counselor, will somehow know how to "appease" this ruler (16:14*b*). Once again we see the premium placed on a wisdom that knows how to control circumstances.

An angry man can cause a lot of harm, destroy property, and even take life, thereby running afoul of the law. He "must pay the penalty" of his misdeeds, and if he is rescued (or released), he will have to be rescued again (19:19). The point is that if the offender's problem is not treated, he will only repeat his performance. Only a changed nature, the new life, can control such a violent spirit. "Anger [indeed] is cruel [or, fierce]" (27:4*a*), but we are given a sure formula to live with a wrathful person— "a gentle answer turns away wrath" (15:1*a*)—and in most instances, the advice works. When it does not, the best recourse is to get out of the way.

Arrogance, insolence, and *unrestrained fury* give us another meaning of wrath (11:4*a*), possibly in the day when God has to judge a person either in this life or the next. A "shameful servant," who performs shoddy work, deserves the wrath of his master, the king (14:35). Certainly the message has great significance for civil servants today in various levels of government when they do not perform well or when they cheat, steal, or lie in their attempt to serve the people. Not only should they be fired, they should also be made to repay what they have taken. All of us need to recapture the meaning of a work ethic that marks us as "wise" employees (14:35*a*). Again, "a bribe concealed in the cloak pacifies great wrath" (21:14*b*). Wisdom does not condone this practice, but merely states the fact that many times even unbelievers know how to pacify the wrath of their fellow man. Finally, we are warned that "wealth is worthless in the day of wrath" (11:4*a*), possibly in the day when God has to judge a person either in this life or the next. Of what use then will be the attempt to offer up our money to atone for our misdeeds?

Another word picture is *annoyance* or *provocation.* "A fool shows his annoyance at once" (12:16*a*) by his outburst of anger when his world does not go the way he wants it. Rather than live "with a quarrelsome and ill-tempered wife" and her frequent outbursts of anger, it is "better to live in" the solitude and peace of the "desert" (21:19). The "provocation by a fool," possibly circumstances that cause him to become angry, is a "heavy" burden (27:3*b*). The figure of trying to lift heavy stones and wet sand (27:3*a*) cannot even come close to the painful anxiety everyone suffers when a fool is aroused.

Another shade of meaning pictures the *one who storms and rages* when he becomes angry. When the king is aroused, his rage is like the roar of a lion (19:12*a*). *Indig-*

nation is another description: the one with "a sly tongue [that is, the backbiter] brings angry looks [or, faces stirred with indignation]" (25:23).

RAGE

One of the most violent of emotions is rage. One form of it describes the "fool [who] is hotheaded" (14:16*b*). Anyone standing near him is well-advised to move out of the way. Because the fool does not know how to put himself under the restraint of God's Word, he can cause problems.

The man who drinks heavily of wine, beer, and even stronger drink is easily aroused, becoming a vile "brawler" (20:1*a*). This word is actually the translation for "intoxicating drink." When a person is controlled by strong drink, he is not aware of the damage he can cause when enraged. Our hearts go out to the family who have to bear this pain and burden when one of their members is a "brawler."

Rage can actually cause a person so aroused to quiver and shake. When "a wise man goes to court with a fool, the fool rages . . . , and there is no peace" for everyone within earshot (29:9). There may be times when it is necessary to rebuke the fool who ignores wisdom, but watch out for the consequences.

SORROW, WOE

Sorrow robs a person of his spirit and brings on deep depression. Any kind of loss—finances, the death of a family member, the waywardness of a son or daughter—can bring sorrow. Yet there are times when we can thank God for such experiences if they bring us closer to the Lord. Sometimes, when we are the most helpless in our sorrow, we have the greatest faith.

By no means should we assume that believers are immune to the emotion of deep sorrow because of loss. When David the king lost his son Absalom, he "was shaken," and as he went to be alone in a room, he wept: "O my son Absalom! . . . If only I had died instead of you—O Absalom, my son, my son" (2 Samuel 18:33). His soul felt sorrow to its very core. We are also sorrowful when we lose loved ones, even if they are believers. But Paul emphasizes the basic key regarding believers in their woe and deep hurt; we do not "grieve like the rest of men, who have *no hope*" (1 Thessalonians 4:13). The sorrow and grief we feel as believers must be measured in the light of eternity because, once we leave this vale of tears, God Himself "will wipe away every tear from [our] eyes" (Revelation 21:4) and we will be reunited with loved ones and friends who preceded us.

As we consider some of the everyday experiences of sorrow, one picture in the book of Proverbs is that of hurt, pain, and possibly injury. The one "who winks maliciously causes grief" (10:10a). He has a way of stirring up strife by the way he acts, and will only suffer loss, either for himself or for those who are in league with him. A much deeper emotion occurs when "the spirit" is crushed by "heartache" (15:13). Any kind of loss can cause a person to temporarily lose his or her drive or ambition. More serious is a lingering or deep depression when the spirit is really broken. Such people may need competent counsel to determine if the problem is spiritual or physical. On the other hand, when a person knows the real blessing of the Lord, he or she is truly "wealthy" and there is no "trouble" in it (10:22). In the Old Testament wealth could be measured in both physical and spiritual blessings; believers today can at least lay hold of "every spiritual blessing" (Ephesians 1:3) so that God can bring joy to the heart.

Grief can make a person sorrowful. The father who has "a fool for a son" knows only grief (17:21a). What enjoyment in life can there be for parents when a mature son or daughter goes astray, turning his or her back on the Lord? This tragedy occurs all too often.

Sorrow comes because of the pain in grief. Even when a person laughs outwardly, "the heart may ache" (14:13) in inward anguish. Sometimes, when we witness to people regarding our faith, we fail to be sensitive with people. They may laugh at our jokes, but inwardly they have sorrow of heart. We need to learn how to be good listeners, trying to draw out what people have in their hearts, even their sorrows and griefs. Then we can truly be used by God to pour the "oil of [genuine] gladness" into the heart and remove the "mourning" and grief (Isaiah 61:3). It takes infinite patience and the wisdom of God to probe the heart of the unbeliever and then provide the "garment of praise" for the "spirit of despair."

Sorrow is also made audible through sighs and groans. "When the wicked rule," that is, when tyrants govern harshly, putting pressure on their subjects, "the people groan" with reason (29:2b). High taxes alone can make people groan loudly. The book of Proverbs also describes the one who has real woe and sorrow: "Those who linger over wine, who go to sample bowls of mixed wine" (23:29-30). They may be trying to drown out their sorrows and miserable existence. When such a person awakes the next morning, however, nothing has changed. The hurt is still there but with greater intensity. Only Jesus takes away our sorrows and removes the burden of despair.

HEAVINESS

"Heaviness" parallels sorrow and grief. One occurrence reflects what we already saw as grief: the son who is foolish, who follows his own ways instead of what wisdom offers, brings "bitterness" to his mother (17:25). No wonder she is heavy-hearted.

An "anxious heart weighs a man down" (12:25a). Perhaps a person faces a crisis in his life, such as an operation or a decision where, if it is wrong, he could lose much. But "a kind word cheers him up" (12:25b) and lifts the burden. Heaviness can also be bitter. Wisdom suggests that wine should be given "to those who are in anguish" (31:6b). In the context, King Lemuel is warned that he must avoid strong drink (31:4-5) to have a clear mind, enabling him to judge rightly. Otherwise, his justice as the leading authority at the highest tribunal might be compromised. On the other hand, in the culture of the day, strong drink was given to those at the point of death, as for example, the person who was condemned and about to perish. And yet, how much better it would be for such a person at the point of death if he were in a better frame of mind. He could receive words of love, comfort, and guidance that would enable him to derive strength from the Word of God. Jesus refused the wine mixed with myrrh because He wanted to leave this life in full command of His faculties (Mark 15:23).

LOATHING

This emotion can be expressed by both the righteous and wicked, depending on the specific circumstances. Most of the passages that describe loathing center on what is abominable. The picture is one of utter revulsion, either on the part of God or man.

"The Lord detests" the wicked person's topsy-turvy way of thinking: "acquitting the guilty and condemning the innocent" (17:15). "The Lord detests the sacrifice of the wicked" (15:8a; 21:27) because their sacrifices reflect only a worship of ritual. Such people may go through the pretense of worship, but their life-style has not changed one iota. They are still the same wicked people. God loathes this insincerity (see also Isaiah 1:11-18). Likewise, even their "prayers are detestable" to the Lord because "they have turned a deaf ear to the law" (28:9). These people refuse to listen and reply with their own words, which are opposite to God's will. Their talk and prayer are considered an abomination.

"The way [and thoughts] of the wicked" are detested by the Lord (15:9a, 26a). Lest we think God is a hard taskmaster, we have to consider why He feels so strongly. The wicked are "proud of heart" (16:5a), have "lying lips" (12:22a), and in their business practices they use "different scales," "different weights and measures," and "differing weights" (11:1a; 20:10a, 23a). Lying and cheating become the mirror by which their entire character is measured. No wonder God detests such people; they flout His absolute standard of righteousness.

In turn, these unbelievers react and declare what they consider undesirable. "Fools detest turning from evil"

(13:19*b*) and become violent with those who seek to help them. The wicked also "detest the upright" (29:27*b*). Conversely, the righteous, or believers, "detest the dishonest" (29:27*a*), including government leaders who "detest wrongdoing" (16:12*a*) as they seek to be honorable. Society, in general, is disgusted with "a mocker" because his "schemes of folly are sin" (24:9). Such mockers may be clever, but they are obnoxious and misapply their intelligence; it will not be long before people seek to condemn these troublemakers.

Another word picture of abhorring is *to be indignant*, similar to a word used for anger. "The mouth of the adulteress is a deep pit" (22:14*a*); she and her customer are, in a sense, "under the Lord's wrath" and "will fall into" this pit (22:14*b*) from which they will never emerge. "The peoples will curse . . . and nations will denounce" those who show partiality "to the guilty" and say to them, "You are innocent" (24:24). Because of common grace, even unbelievers have a perception of justice and become angry when they see its miscarriage benefit the wicked.

In one curious aspect of abhorrence, the wicked "bring shame" (lit., cause a bad odor) when they lie (13:5). The words of liars not only move the air but foul it up, assaulting everyone's senses. Wisdom has a graphic way of pointing out how hideous is wrong-doing and, by such means, seeks to curb wickedness.

ENVY

Envy can cause many problems, and even believers are not immune if they stray from the Lord. The picture of envy includes jealousy, being zealous in an evil sense, exciting to anger, and provocation.

The one whose "heart [is] at peace" can experience health and life in "the body," but a person can become ill when consumed by envy because it will rot "the bones" (14:30). Wisdom seeks to encourage people not to let the "heart envy sinners" for what they have, "but always be zealous for the fear of the Lord" (23:17). We are warned "not [to] envy wicked men" or "desire their company"

(24:1, 19). The sons of Korah had excellent counsel to share: it is better to be "a doorkeeper in the house of the Lord than to dwell in the tents of the wicked" (Psalm 84:10), enjoying their dainties.

Last comes the warning against immorality. "Anger is cruel and fury overwhelming, but who can stand before jealousy?" (27:4). The man who commits adultery is in danger of losing his life at the hands of a husband whose wife was caught in her sin. Society generally understands the fury of such a husband when his frenzied jealousy prompts him to actually kill the man who committed adultery with his wife.

HATRED

Another of man's consuming passions, even more than envy, is hatred. Out of the innermost springs of a person's heart erupts this emotion, and too often it is not quelled before the most terrible violence has been committed.

One key word, used thirteen times to depict hatred, conveys the picture of a person who bears a grudge or cherishes an animosity that can break out at any time in violence: "Bloodthirsty men hate a man of integrity and seek to kill the upright" (29:10).

The person "who hates correction" is actually regarded as "stupid" (12:1b). In the long run he "will die" if he does not listen to wisdom (15:10b). "A poor man is shunned [lit., hated] by all his relatives" (19:7a), probably because he is an embarrassment to them. Too often believers shut their ears and eyes to fellow believers who are poor.

Some hate others but are careful not to reveal it. Instead, they cover their inner feelings with gracious words, but in their hearts they harbor deceit (26:24). "A lying tongue hates those it hurts, and a flattering tongue works ruin" in the end (26:28). "The accomplice of a thief is his own enemy [lit., hates his soul or life]" (29:24a), possibly because he is not in sympathy with what the thief is doing but cannot evade the offender's clutches.

Believers should dislike wrong-doing intensely. The one who "refuses [lit., hates] to strike hands in pledge [that is, guarantee loans] is safe" (11:15b) from this horrendous burden. "The righteous hate what is false (13:5a). The one "who hates bribes will live" (15:27b) and not suffer any ill consequences, as when Elisha refused Naaman's gifts (2 Kings 5:15-16). In a similar vein, wisdom's counsel is that "he who hates ill-gotten wealth will enjoy a long life" (28:16).

Some timely advice is also provided: "seldom set foot in the neighbor's house—too much of you, and he will hate you" (25:17). The pointed warning is that a believer should not wear out his welcome by continually disrupting his host's everyday routine.

Wisdom also indicates that the parent who "spares the rod" hates his son or daughter (13:24a). Failure to discipline one's children actually reflects a lack of concern for them.

FEAR

Fear is an emotion that has both positive and negative effects. It can be devastating, but it can also bring true riches when there is reverence for the Lord. Fourteen times in Proverbs the idea of reverence for the Lord is mentioned where, in a sense, we acknowledge the claim God has on our lives (see chapter 8).

By no means are these all the human emotions the book of Proverbs mentions. A healthy emotional life is a moral and spiritual life when the heart is in right relationship with God. Modern psychology tries to produce a proper emotional life by helping people to adjust to their environment. But within the human being is a fallen nature that dogs and undermines him: only an alignment with God can give a person the new life that will provide emotional stability. The believer in right relationship with the Lord is the best possible type of citizen in today's society.

He who fears the Lord has a secure fortress,
and for his children it will be a refuge.

Proverbs 14:26

A wife of noble character who can find?
She is worth far more than rubies.

Proverbs 31:10

A wise son [or daughter] brings joy to his [or her] father,
but a foolish man [or woman] despises his [or her] mother.

Proverbs 15:20

10

RELATIONSHIPS WITHIN THE FAMILY

A major topical study in Proverbs pertains to what is desirable for the best possible relationships within the family, the smallest unit of society established by God. Therefore, wisdom desires to give guidance to everyone within this unit (see chapter 4). In a day of apparent sophistication and civilization, we still have many unresolved problems within the family. The divorce rate is now 50 percent. Divorces among Christian couples—almost unheard of only a generation ago—are on the rise. And when Christians remarry, pastors and church leaders face real problems as to what to do with these people in the local congregation.

While clergymen, psychologists, social workers, and marriage counselors grope for answers, the book of Proverbs, collected and written almost three thousand years ago, remains an up-to-date authority with basic advice on how to stabilize the family. If these instructions are followed, parents and children will have meaningful relationships. Children can be encouraged to know the Lord, serve Him, and, as a result, serve society with the greatest capacities of usefulness.

THE FAMILY IN GENERAL

Proverbs clearly identifies the family as pivotal for society because of the fifth commandment (Exodus 20:12). There, the guideline of an absolute ethic requires children to honor their father and mother. Proverbs expands on this commandment: the value of family loyalties is to be treasured; children are to be reared in accordance with instruction provided by God; the loving bond between generations is encouraged so that grandchildren "are a crown to the aged [that is, the grandparents] and parents are the pride of their children" (17:6). Lest anyone think that this instruction was for the Old Testament world only, Paul repeats the fifth commandment in the New Testament: "Children, obey your parents in the Lord, for this is right. 'Honor your father and mother'—which is the first commandment with a promise—'that it may go well with you and that you may enjoy long life on the earth'" (Ephesians 6:1-3).

Proverbs clearly defines the norm for a family as the union of one husband and one wife. As we have already seen, the husband is encouraged to be loyal to and "captivated by" his wife's love (5:19c). For a woman to break her marriage vow is to sin against the "partner of her youth" and thereby "ignore the covenant she made before God" (2:17). This is a far cry from some of the examples of polygamy in the Old Testament, involving even David and Solomon. Perhaps the latter, because of his many wives, came to value the wisdom of one wife for one husband as foundational to the best family relationships.

The wife is no mere second-rate person, as commonly thought in the ancient pagan world. Wisdom's advice is that the wife can actually make or undo her husband: "he who finds a wife finds what is good" (18:22a); the "prudent wife is from the Lord" (19:14b); and "a wife of noble character is her husband's crown, but a disgraceful wife is like decay in his bones" (12:4).

Family stability depends on the wisdom of a good wife who seeks the best for her home: she "builds her house" (14:1a); her exceptional gifts are always to be recognized and accepted in the community; "her husband has full confidence in her and lacks nothing of value"; "give her the reward she has earned, and let her works bring her praise at the city gate [that is, where the city council sits]" (31:11, 31). All of these guidelines were intended to set forth a high view of the family, and any deviation, particularly in sexual sin, was portrayed in the darkest of hues (see again 5:9-14 and 6:24-33).

CHILDREN IN GENERAL

One of the greatest blessings in life is when a father and mother await their first-born. At the birth of the child, the parents dote with ecstasy on their infant boy or girl. In an even greater way, grandparents can be hilarious as they lavish affection on their grandchildren. Children in general are a blessing of the Lord, and Solomon could beam with pride as he wrote, "Blessed is the man whose quiver is full of them" (Psalm 127:5), that is, when he has his many children about him. A number of psalms are classified as wisdom psalms, but the wisdom of Proverbs also emphasizes the blessed position children have within the family.

"A good man [that is, one who is moral and upright], leaves an inheritance to his children's children (13:22a). It is far more desirable to have a good name than to have ill-gotten riches, which leave a rotten testimony that children have to bear in shame.

We observe again the important function the fear of the Lord plays in family relationships: "He who fears the Lord has a secure fortress" (14:26a), that is, when the father places great trust in God's power and has a keen respect for His word. When he follows this guideline for his life and family, "his secure fortress . . . will be a refuge . . . for his children" (14:26b). Blessed are parents who build such values into the hearts of their offspring.

While grandparents consider grandchildren to be their most precious crown, young people take pride and glory in the achievements of their parents (17:6). What child, when he has reason, has not boasted of his father to his playmates, only to hear from his companions an equally vivid description?

"Even a child [generally, teenager, from the Hebrew *na'ar*] is known by his actions, by whether his conduct is pure and right" (20:11). His conduct will generally reflect the influences to which he has been exposed. Are they wholesome and uplifting to produce traits that are good and right? Even the teenager, while struggling for his or her sense of identity and independence, still desires inwardly the guidance that will be for his or her good. When grown, wise children will display the positive emotions in chapter 9 and make true the proverb that the "father of a righteous" and wise son "has great joy" (23:24-25). The father and mother will be glad to see their offspring serving the Lord and being useful members of society.

THE FATHER

LOVING INSTRUCTION

The "wise son heeds his father's instructions" (13:1). How precious is the home where the father takes the time to correct his children in the manner as directed by the Word of God. If the child learns early his boundaries, he will grow up to enjoy the greatest freedom. If our children and young people learn to avoid the pitfalls of life, its immoralities and vices, they will not become enslaved to bad habits. They will be free to choose the ways of the Lord.

The child is further encouraged to "listen to [his] father who gave [him] life" (23:22*a*). The word "listen" is in the imperative. Wisdom actually commands the child to listen to his father, who serves and stands in the place of God as the authority figure. But the father is not a tyrant; rather, the good father knows how to be a loving person and still keep a firm hand on his young brood.

Wisdom gently reminds the son and daughter not to turn from good advice. "Stop listening to instruction [or, discipline], my son, and you will stray from the words of knowledge" (19:27). Today, advice comes from all quarters by all kinds of people, but unless they adhere to a

standard provided by the Word of God, young people will
go astray.

The son and daughter are also advised to be "wise,"
to follow the guidelines provided in Scripture by keeping
their "heart on the right path" (23:19). The young are to
willingly give their hearts (that is, give undivided attention) to what is taught by wisdom through the father or
formal teacher (23:26a). They will then be able to guard
their ways for godly and moral living and take delight in a
personal experience with the Lord. "Eat honey, my son [or
daughter], for it is good; honey from the comb is sweet to
your taste" (24:13). What child has to be told twice to eat
cake or candy? But the appeal to eat sweet honey also
drives home a precious truth: "Know also that wisdom is
sweet to your soul; if you find it, there is a future hope for
you, and your hope will not be cut off" (24:14). The greatest of all pleasures is gained when pursuing wisdom, and
the son or daughter who determines to do so will find
hope for the future, honor in old age, and reward in the
world to come.

FATHER OF THE GOOD SON

Parents and counselors put much emphasis today on
the vocations children should follow: football player,
teacher, engineer, doctor, business executive, clothes de-
signer, and so on. But no matter what pursuit in life one
chooses, God places top priority on the son or daughter
who is wise, not in mere intellectual knowledge, but in
the *moral* grasp wisdom provides (10:1; 13:1; 15:20;
17:25). No matter what vocation one follows in life, a godly moral standard needs to be exercised that will impact
society on its many levels.

When the young become adults and begin to make
their mark among people, they are reminded that "a wise
son brings joy to his father, but a foolish son brings grief to
his mother" (10:1). The two lines are an excellent example of an antithetic parallelism. Note the opposites: wise
and foolish; father and mother; joy and grief. The wise offspring should take the path provided by wisdom, which

leads to right conduct before the Lord. Furthermore, when the heart is right, a unique moral character will shape by excellence the vocation the son or daughter chooses to follow.

When the "wise son brings joy to his father," no greater reward can exist for parents. Such joy is in the superlative degree because the word for it is inward excitement (see chapter 9). Even though a man can be used greatly by God in the lives of many people, his greatest joy comes when his own children walk in the ways of the Lord. Parents whose believing sons and daughters are living for the Lord have the greatest reason to be hilarious in their praise to God.

The "wise son heeds his father's instruction [or, correction]" (13:1). Actually, "heeds" is not in the original language. We can best understand the verse to mean that the offspring will *become* wise by the efforts of the father. Through example and loving discipline, the father has to teach his son or daughter the right way. No parent should expect the schools of today to do what is his or her God-given right: to teach biblical morals.

The person who "keeps [or, guards for himself] the law [that is, divine instruction] is a discerning son" (28:7a). Obviously, the idea of this passage can be misused and turned into something legalistic, but such an emphasis is not the intent. Wisdom points out that when sons or daughters keep for themselves the scriptural instruction of their wise parents or teachers, they will not only have opportunity to know the Lord but will also follow Him all the days of their lives as people with moral discernment.

FATHER OF THE EVIL SON

Unfortunately many passages also depict the sorrow brought upon the father by evil offspring. No doubt, this is wisdom's way of pointing out to the family what to avoid in order to emphasize the more desirable way.

"A foolish son brings grief to his father" (17:25; also see chapter 9). The word "grief" reflects the picture of vexation, even anger. In a feeling of helplessness about a wayward son or daughter, the father may cry out, "Why did this happen to me?"

"A foolish son is his father's ruin" (19:13a) pictures the ruin as an empty chasm. Wayward children can leave parents feeling empty. The same word also reflects calamity or disaster. So serious are the devious involvements of such offspring, another shade of meaning pictures the father's emotional state in terms of having the taste of sour wine in his mouth.

The son who would rob or assault his father "brings shame and disgrace" (19:26). Imagine the horror felt by a father subjected to this abuse. Yet, in our permissive society, these things can and do happen.

The child who is "a companion of gluttons disgraces his father" (28:7b). Overeating at banquets is not the only vice to which wisdom points. The problem is deeper because the son squanders his hard-earned money to indulge only himself. What is shameful is that he keeps company with the wrong crowd, drinks, and will eventually be caught in antisocial acts that will shame his father. Many in our generation have not learned the value of self-control and the virtue of self-discipline. These good and desirable values are based on God's righteousness.

Sometimes payment comes back in kind. When a foolish and rebellious son or daughter grows up and has a family of his own, and when his or her own children turn out to be rebellious, the lessons of wisdom are learned the hard way. Wisdom wants to spare both parents and children such grief.

THE MOTHER

In biblical context, the father and mother are a unit, and after considering specific lessons regarding the father, wisdom carefully takes the time to also describe the mother's position and role in the family.

THE MOTHER OF THE GOOD SON

Chapter 1 has already reminded us that the mother is directly involved in the training of a child (1:8). The Scriptures point out a number of wives and mothers who were godly and well-versed in the Word: Hannah (1 Samuel 2:1-10), Abigail (1 Samuel 25), and Mary (Luke 1:45-55), to mention only a few.

A curious statement concerns the oracle, or burden, that King Lemuel received from his mother (31:1). We are not sure who King Lemuel was, but Jewish sources identify him with Solomon. (See the discussion in chapter 1 for a possible identification of Lemuel.) If so, the mother who is giving her words of instruction is none other than Bathsheba who, by the time Solomon was about to become king over Israel, had become a much wiser woman. She knew only too well from her personal experience the temptations to which kings could easily fall prey. She warned Solomon against the sins of drunkenness and sexual overindulgence. While her warnings are quite pointed (31:3-9), her counsel is balanced by the wise advice concerning the model wife (31:10-31). The entire chapter has just the kind of advice any godly woman should give to her son or daughter about to embark on life's journey.

THE MOTHER OF THE EVIL SON

Wisdom warns again of the tragic results of wrong decisions by the evil son or daughter. No doubt, the child or teenager is reminded that if he follows a foolish life-style, his or her wrong choices will be keenly felt by the mother. "A foolish son [is a] grief to this mother" (10:1). How many wayward sons or daughters have caused gray hairs for a mother? Parenthood has great blessings, but the possibility also exists for pain and suffering, and the mother feels it keenly when children go astray.

A wayward son can actually drive "his mother" out of the home (19:26a). When the son robs his father, the mother simply cannot take the contention and strife and runs away. Pity the poor mother who has to suffer the anguish of exile from her own home to get away from the uproar of one or more godless offspring. A mother may also know the experience of "disgrace" because of a son or daughter who has not been properly disciplined: "The rod of correction imparts wisdom" (29:15a).

It is frightful to think of mothers who have been made ill, have grown old before their time, or have gone to an untimely death because of wayward, rebellious children. We need to consider carefully and try to understand what it means to carry the burden of how a mother feels as she has had to endure the untimely death of a child who has refused to listen to her word of advice. We should take seriously this matter of teaching our children wisdom from the Word to prepare them for what they will have to face in the years ahead.

CORRECTION AND DISCIPLINE

Fathers and mothers of today's generation find it difficult to discipline their children. Capricious discipline is out of the question, as spanking for any reason or hurting the unruly child for the slightest provocation. Yet discipline is necessary, and parents should take seriously this guidance by wisdom for rearing children. There is a time for gentle reprimand and withholding of privileges, but when every other means for discipline has been exhausted, then wisdom points out the use of the switch in the woodshed. Some young people today can be provocative and brash, defy the authority of either parents or society's leaders, break the law, and cause untold harm in the community. Such rebellious behavior, however, can be traced back to lack of discipline in the home. Permissiveness has bred a generation of law-breakers. Two sets of discipline are described: one of general application to the son or daughter, and the other specifically for teenagers.

TRAINING THE SON OR DAUGHTER

No actual age is indicated here, but generally we would assume that the child is a preteen. Wisdom instructs that the parent "who spares the rod hates his son [or daughter]," but real love necessitates the use of discipline in child training (13:24). Parents may find it more loving to avoid hard discipline, but, in the long run the father or mother will grow to hate his or her child if the neglect of discipline leads to rebellious conduct in later life. Wisdom directs that the training process should begin *early* in life.

A further warning indicates that "a wise servant will rule [that is, be given preference in the family inheritance rights] over a disgraceful son" (17:2). In the culture of that day, servants were used in the home for a number of tasks, but if the wayward son did not mend his ways, he may have found himself subservient to the very servant he grew up with in earlier life.

The son or daughter is to be disciplined while there "is hope" (19:18a). The picture for "discipline" is suggestive of corporal punishment. Moreover, the directive to parents is given as a command: "Discipline your son" (19:18a). The word does suggest an option that can be avoided. Why? When the child is young and impressionable, there is hope for improvement. The tree can only be bent while it is young; once grown, it can no longer be shaped. So with the child. If the child grows up to be a rebellious person, only the Lord can produce a radical change in his nature and heart.

As for the phrase "Do not be a willing party to his death" (19:18b), two possibilities for interpretation are suggested. One is that care should be exercised that death does not result from disciplinary action. The other is that discipline should be applied early in life to prevent a child from wayward or reckless behavior that may someday result in violent death or the imposition of the death penalty (Deuteronomy 21:18-21). Both have merit for consideration, but the second suggestion carries the greater weight. The King James Version has "and let not thy soul spare for his crying" (19:18b), but this may not be the best translation.

The instruction for correction is repeated: "discipline your son, and he will give you peace; he will bring delight to your soul" (29:17). The word "discipline" is the same one as in 19:18, given again in the command form. The point is that when necessary the son needs to be disciplined for his own good, either as sharp reproof or corporal punishment. If the parent is faithful, the son or daughter will become a moral and spiritual adult.

TRAINING THE TEENAGER

Previously, the discipline was to be applied without specific reference to age. However, the word "child" in the passages now to be considered refers generally to the teenage years, though we cannot be dogmatic about it in every context.

We have already discussed the desirable conduct by the teenager in 4:1, 5:7, and 7:24, but the first occurrence of this word in chapters 10-31 is in the well-known passage in chapter 22: "Train a child [that is, the teenager] in the way he should go, and when he is old he will not turn from it" (22:6). The idea of "train" is to dedicate or make experienced, and it appears in the form of a command. The parent may not shirk his responsibility, particularly with a teenager who actually needs his father's guidance *as much as* a toddler.

Such training implies two possibilities: (1) to provide the adolescent with habits anchored to a moral standard, or (2) to help the teenager realize in his or her own way the training that best fits his or her physical and mental capacity. The former is probably what wisdom has as a goal. When the teen becomes an adult, the promise is that the moral training will remain with him or her all through life. This statement is given as a general truth.

Unfortunately, in spite of the best of parental training and example, there are times when the teenager will turn out wrong and drift far from the Lord. However, the promise of hope is there; it might take a lifetime, in some instances, for a wayward person with all the advantages of a good background to return to what he was taught. Most of the time, he will come back. All God asks is that parents be faithful in accordance with the teaching of the Scriptures.

Another word from wisdom reminds us that "folly is bound up in the heart of a child" (22:15a). In the company of his peers the teen may commit acts of disobedience and other antisocial behavior he or she might not do if by himself. The remedy? Wisdom tells us that "the rod of discipline [that is, correction] will drive it [folly or foolishness] far from him" (22:15*b*). If verbal admonition does not help, then physical discipline is necessary.

"The rod of correction [or, reproof, argument] imparts wisdom" (29:15*a*) to the teenager, and sometimes this is the only way an adolescent fellow or girl can learn. But if there is no discipline and the teenager is "left to himself," (29:15*b*), that is, sent away without punishment, he or she will in the long run disgrace his or her mother.

Some educators and child psychologists deplore any hand laid on a child or a young person. Obviously, severe discipline is a court of last appeal, but parents who refuse to use it at all will suffer the consequences in the end, having contributed an incorrigible and evil element to society. Fathers and mothers must take time with their children, really know them, encourage an atmosphere of complete trust. With healthy, open interpersonal communication, the young person will more likely accept the verbal correction and sometimes sharp reproof. Parents, however, should follow through with their discipline, and not just yell and threaten. To shout and not actually discipline is just good advice with no teeth. Parents need all the wisdom they can get, but the Word of God provides it, and when a mother and father are faithful to its directives, children can grow up to be believers, love their parents, and also serve society usefully.

CHARACTER OF A WAYWARD SON OR DAUGHTER

Even the best of training is no guarantee that wisdom will be instilled in every child. Out of a good home can come a lazy person ("he who sleeps during harvest"; 10:5*b*) and even an immoral child who is a "companion of prostitutes" (29:3*b*). Godly parents can have children who, as "mockers," are too obstinate in their ways to "listen to rebuke" (13:1*b*). Out of the best of homes can come foolish people who "do not bless their mothers" (30:11*b*), who rob "father or mother" of their money (28:24*a*), and who even drive the mother from the house (19:26*a*). The list is horrible to comprehend, but the book of Proverbs "tells it like it is."

Some parents have only themselves to blame for their "disgrace" because they refuse to correct their off-spring (29:15). However, the rebellious son (or daughter) also has to bear the judgment. Such a one will be held responsible for being a "companion of prostitutes" (29:3*a*), and his or her consent to do evil sets the course. But the faithful parent may live to see his son or daughter brought to the Lord after passing through many trials and sorrows, or the repentance of rebellious children may take place years after the parents are gone. The ten or fifteen years children are entrusted to the parents for child training pass all too quickly. How we as parents need His wisdom to do the best job possible.

BROTHERS

Not many passages in Proverbs deal with this word, although it must be remembered that the Hebrew word for "brother" can be used of the wider family constituency: cousins, and other relatives.

Poor relatives and friends are always unpopular: "A poor man is shunned by all his relatives—how much more do his friends avoid him! Though he pursues them with pleading, they are nowhere to be found" (19:7). Ancient injustices are unfortunately all too often modern ones as well. "An offended brother is more unyielding than a fortified city, and disputes are like the barred gates of a citadel" (18:19). Feuds that result from these situations may lead to a lasting bitterness that spans several generations. Rightly does wisdom declare that these contentions are like the "barred gates of a citadel [or, castle]," so strong that it is difficult to break them.

On the other hand, healthy relationships can also exist within the family. A friend can love at all times and give substantial help when necessary. In times of crises, however, families can close ranks, and a brother can be especially helpful. The saying of the modern proverb is true—blood is thicker than water—and in times of testing one can rely on his kin. Yet there are times when the services of a friend, rather than a brother, are more desirable. The particular situation will determine which avenue to pursue for aid.

On those occasions where it is necessary to turn to the friend, wisdom does point out that "there is a friend that sticks closer than a brother" (18:24a) and "better a neighbor nearby than a brother far away" (27:10c). Generally, no man lives on an island by himself, and when those special times of need come, friends can be God-given.

Kings take pleasure in honest lips;
they value a man who speaks the truth.

Proverbs 16:13

The sluggard buries his hand in the dish;
he will not even bring it back to his mouth.

Proverbs 19:24

Do not answer a fool according to his folly,
or you will be like him yourself.

Proverbs 26:4

11

SPEECH, LAZINESS, AND FOLLY

The book of Proverbs is God's wisdom applied to the needs of ordinary people in everyday life. To be wise is to follow such guidance for everyday affairs. In chapter 8 wisdom provided insight into how God and man need to relate to one another. Chapter 9 dealt with our emotions. Excellent advice was given in chapter 10 for the best possible family relations. In this chapter we consider how wisdom (1) guides the formation of the thoughts in our hearts into words, (2) describes for us how lazy people live and act (at the same time directing us in how to make the best use of the time God provides), and (3) warns us of fools who have little use for the things of God and know only how to produce strife and contention.

SPEECH

Three separate words are used by wisdom to describe various kinds of talk: a *word*, a *matter*, and a *thing*. Seven subtopics are considered.

HOW THE WICKED USE WORDS

The words evil people use serve as a warning to us: "The words of the wicked lie in wait for blood" (12:6a).

These people have committed great time and effort in planning how to shed the blood of the innocent. They either plot how to do it themselves or use other people to accomplish their objectives.

We are enjoined against eating "the food of a stingy man [lit., person with an evil eye]" (23:6a). Such an individual has no concern for his guests, and those who dine with him "will vomit up the little" that was eaten. Any "compliments" given the stingy person will only be "wasted" (23:8).

In addition, we are advised not to "envy wicked men" or "desire their company. . . . Their lips talk [only] about making trouble" (24:1-2b). These scoundrels may appear to be successful, but in the end their ill-gotten gains will only have the Lord's condemnation. God "frustrates [or, overturns] the words of the unfaithful" because of his plots against those with the "knowledge of God's word" (22:12). Believers have to be constantly on guard against those who have little or no use for godly people.

CARE IN USING WORDS

God's words of instruction must always be keenly regarded and obeyed. "He who scorns instruction [lit., the word] will pay for it" (13:13a). The "word" is a reference to the moral law or divine commandments (sometimes related to the "Ten Words," or Decalogue). The one who ignores or despises them puts himself in debt to God, and will have to answer for his disobedience. In the antithetic parallel of the verse, "he who respects [or, fears] a command [or, the commandment]" and seeks to do it with his whole heart "is rewarded" (13:13b).

We must not argue with a fool because, if we try to use the wisdom that comes from the Word of God, the fool will only despise it. He will not be inclined to appreciate "the wisdom of your words" (23:9). On the other hand, a wise teacher or godly parent "will be glad" and "rejoice" when our "lips speak what is right" (23:15b-16). As already indicated, wisdom leads her disciples to the right course in life (1:2-3). God, therefore, wants our lips to speak only what is in conformity to His revealed Word. We are not to "add to [God's] words" (30:6a). "Every word of God is flawless" (30:5a) and tested as silver. But when we add to the Word the precepts and interpretations of men, contrary to His spoken Word, He "will rebuke . . . and prove" us to be liars (30:6b). Traditions are all right if they explain accurately what God intends. But traditions have a way of multiplying themselves and often end up twisting and perverting what God had originally intended.

Proverbs warns against talking too much because, sooner or later, "sin is not absent" (10:19a), or colloquially, "You'll put your foot in your mouth." The old saying is true: after we speak a word, it can rule over us; but before we speak the word, we are the ruler of that word. In the latter sense, as long as the word has not been spoken, we can still shape it until it conforms to what God desires of good speech.

On the other hand, when verbally attacked, the "gentle answer turns away wrath" (15:1a). Mild and peaceable speech often averts a quarrel, "but a harsh word stirs up anger" (15:1b). How delightful when "a man finds joy in giving an apt reply—and how good is a timely word" (15:23). Most people will welcome a wise word spoken at the right moment.

The man "who speaks the truth [that is, what is morally straight]" (16:13b) will be valued by all who listen. Even unbelievers will recognize what is right and will generally have respect for such a person. On the other hand, "a man who speaks in haste [lit., is hasty with his words]" (29:20a) will have cause for regret. Unfortunately, he does not stop to think of what he is saying and then acts impetuously. "There is more hope for a fool than for him" (29:20b).

"The words of a man's mouth are deep waters" (18:4a). The use of the metaphor "deep waters" refers to the necessary practice of hauling water up from deep wells where it was cold and uncontaminated. When we research the background of this proverb, we can understand why wisdom chose such a picture to describe the pure and righteous words of the wise man. We are further reminded that wise words generally do not come hastily. They are well thought out and require time and effort to find just· the right words for appropriate occasions.

Another possibility of understanding the passage is derived from the parallel in the second line of the verse: right and wise words are as a "bubbling brook," which comes from "the fountain of wisdom" (18:4b). As the water of a brook continually bubbles forth, there is very little possibility of stagnation. Words, therefore, that come from the wisdom of God are free from pollution and flow without ceasing.

WORD OF ENCOURAGEMENT OR INSTRUCTION

"An anxious heart weighs a man down" (12:25a). Anxiety as a negative emotion can be extremely depressing—and feel as heavy as a load of stones. But what a privilege we have, when we see a neighbor's spirit sagging, to speak "a kind word," a word of sympathy or encouragement that will cheer him up (12:25b) and give him hope. The right words give a person the strength to continue on in the face of adversity. As believers, we should seize the many opportunities to encourage unbelievers and through this testimony perhaps to point such a one to Christ, who has the ultimate power to lift burdens.

The naive or inexperienced person, generally the teenager who has not yet had the opportunity to test the options in life, will tend to believe every word he hears (14:15a). However, the "prudent man [or woman] gives thought to his [her] steps" (14:15b). The prudent person has matured in the Lord so as to sift carefully what is heard and consider wisely the course·in life that will glorify God and be the greatest help to society. By knowing how to accept right words, the sensible person will find true happiness.

The encouragement to the naive is to turn their ears and "listen to the sayings [lit., words] of the wise"

(22:17*b*) so that they can have the knowledge of God. The godly teacher has the right to ask his disciples to "apply" his or her "heart" to the words that come from the Lord. This is the knowledge that will enable the naive person to "trust . . . in the Lord" (22:19*a*) and then give further opportunity to use the options that will make him or her wise in this world.

As a conclusion to the emphasis on the use of "word" or "matter," wisdom instructs that "a word aptly spoken," at the right time and in the proper circumstances, will be "like apples of gold in settings of silver" (25:11). This word picture could refer to the practice of molding forms in the shape of apples made of gold and set as ornaments in a silver carving on the top of the columns of a building. But whatever the picture is intended to convey, it defines what is considered extremely precious. As these metals represent great value, so are words spoken by a wise person at the right time—words that will affect people and encourage them to turn to the Lord. God's wisdom, far from being theoretical or rationalistic, as was Greek philosophy, enables people to live practical and godly lives in a way that will have a powerful bearing upon people in every generation.

THE MOUTH

The book of Proverbs has much to say about the mouth—about the words that come from the mouths of both the evil and the righteous.

Right words. Wisdom places a great premium on the use of right words: "From the fruit of his lips [lit., mouth] a man is filled with good things" (12:14*a*). Wise words and good advice bring a sense of satisfaction to the one who utters them because the good he does will come back to him. "From the fruit of his lips a man enjoys [lit., eats] good things" (13:2*a*). A proper use of the mouth will in the long run serve him well, and people will respect the righteous man for his few but well-chosen wise words.

Even if words are pure and righteous, excessive talk will only detract from a good man's testimony. Wisdom warns a person to "guard his lips" because, in the long run, he will "guard his soul" (13:3a). This verse repeats what has already been mentioned: too often, with the use of many words, "sin is not absent," and such a blabberer "will come to ruin" (13:3b). The one "who holds his tongue is wise" (10:19b). The key, therefore, for proper behavior is the right use of words at the proper time—and no more.

"The fruit of a person's mouth"—that is, his speech —will fill his "stomach" and his inner being (18:20a). "With the harvest from his lips he is satisfied" (18:20b). The choice of right words brings a sense of gratification.

Evil talk. By contrast, the wrong use of the mouth can also perpetrate wrong deeds: "The mouth of the wicked gushes evil" (15:28b). The man or woman who has an evil tongue does not stop to think but rather pours forth what is present in his or her heart, adversely affecting many in society. The wrong use of the mouth, declares wisdom, wreaks its devastation: while "the head of the righteous" is crowned with "blessings" (10:6a), "violence overwhelms the mouth of the wicked" (10:6b), a pointed description that is repeated in 10:11b. The second line of these passages is a word picture describing how violence covers the entire countenance, particularly the mouth. In a sense, the wicked need to cover their faces, and especially their mouths, in the presence of the righteous because their words have been so foul. Note what happened to the wicked Haman when the king's guard covered his face after all his evil deeds came to light (Esther 7:8). In a somewhat similar vein: "the mouth of the righteous is a fountain of life" (10:11a) because from his mouth comes forth everything that encourages and helps. "The mouth of the wicked," however, spews forth all manner of evil (10:11b).

Again, from "the lips of the righteous" comes what "is fitting," but from "the mouth of the wicked only what is perverse" (10:32), which disrupts and destroys everything that is decent. Wisdom even says that the "perverse tongue" should be cut out (10:31b). The picture is quite pointed: an evil tongue must be stopped at all costs before any further damage is committed against society.

Words can be devastating. The "mouth [of] the godless destroys his neighbor" (11:9a), but on an even greater scale, the "mouth of the wicked" can cause conflict within a city, resulting in its destruction (11:11b). Such speech needs to be completely silenced. Worse yet is what can happen within a fellowship of believers. Some carnal Christians need only open their mouths, and factions will polarize, people will be deeply hurt, and a full-scale fight can erupt. Believers need to be wary of suggestions offered by people out of God's will and must stand ready to eliminate any disagreement that has a potential for splitting the fellowship.

"Food [or, wealth] gained by fraud tastes sweet" (20:17a) at first. But retribution comes sooner or later, and what was once enjoyed will eventually be as palatable as "a mouth full of gravel" (20:17b). Ill-gotten gain obtained by outright stealing or through other more subtle means seems clever (see 1:13-14), but the one who lives a life of falsehood will, in the long run, taste bitterness not only in his mouth but in his heart and soul as well.

Once again, immorality becomes an issue. The mouth that only knows how to flatter for personal, selfish reasons brings destruction, and we should be on guard when faced by such talk. The adulterous woman flatters with evil intent; her "mouth . . . is a deep pit" (22:14b). She is not even aware of the evil brought about by her words, and after her immoral involvement she only "eats and wipes her mouth and says, 'I've done nothing wrong'" (30:20b-c).

Wisdom commends the good use of the mouth. While "the words of the wicked lie in wait for blood" for their intended victim, "the speech [lit., mouth] of the upright rescues them" (12:6). Righteous people should speak out against unjust deeds; those who commit crime must not get away from the consequences of their evil. Sometimes in our legal systems today, offenders seemingly merit better treatment than the victim or his family, and if the proper balance of justice is not restored, law and order will break down further.

Fools and their words. Wisdom makes a special point of how fools use their mouths. "Wise men" know how to "store up knowledge," but foolish folk talk without thinking and have no regard for the way they use words. When the fool opens his mouth, "ruin" is at hand (10:14b) for himself and others, resulting in grief and loss. To minimize the tragedy, wisdom suggests that "a fool's talk" merits "a rod to his back" (lit., "in the mouth of the foolish is a rod of pride"; 14:3a). The word for "rod" occurs both here and in Isaiah 11:1, where it is translated: "A 'shoot' will come up from the stump of Jesse." As it is applied in 14:3a, a shoot is growing out of the mouth of the foolish that makes his foolish speech grotesque. In another sense, however, this rod of pride becomes the means by which the fool receives a beating because of his arrogant talk and proud words. The fool should learn how to keep a guard over his lips instead of feeding "on folly" (15:14b).

Leaders and their words. Leaders of a nation must ever be careful how they use their mouths. In the Old Testament, the king was God's regent, and when he spoke, it was as if God rendered His decision for the nation Israel. Therefore, the king had to be careful that "his mouth should not betray justice" (16:10b). He was under obligation not to pervert God's justice. Too often, however, Judah's kings paid no attention to God's wisdom. Likewise, many today in civil leadership overturn justice and sin with their evil mouths.

The mother who taught King Lemuel could have been none other than Bathsheba (see Introduction). The words she shared with her son as he was about to become king (31:1-9) are quite pointed: He must be the champion of "those who cannot speak for themselves, for the rights of all who are destitute [lit., sons of passing away]" (31:8). He had to "speak up and judge fairly; defend the rights of the poor and needy" (31:9). The idea of "sons passing away" pictures men in their frail humanity; they need to have at least one individual who can champion their rights and give them comfort in the midst of a life beset by oppression.

The righteous king, representing God as the true King, was to help defenseless people who desperately needed protection. People in civil leadership today must realize that their decisions are no less important than in days long ago for kings in Israel. They should not only reflect the wisest of the people who elected them but, even more important, the righteousness of the King of the whole earth. Civil authorities who feather their own nests at the expense of the people they seek to serve will find that they have to give an account to God for their evil ways.

The godly woman. The discussion on the right use of the mouth closes with the speech of the godly woman: "she speaks [lit., opens her mouth] with wisdom and faithful instruction [lit., law of kindness] is on her tongue" (31:26). Her words of instruction reflect a godly common sense, and her children and neighbors benefit from her speech and example.

HOW ONE SHOULD ANSWER

Four passages in the book of Proverbs specify how one should reply in response to life's situations. The way we answer can reflect either God's wisdom or human folly.

"The heart of the righteous weighs its answers" (15:28a) for each specific circumstance because he has learned to ponder well before he speaks. In contrast, the "rich man answers harshly" (18:23b) when confronted by a poor person who "pleads for mercy" in his or her desperate need (18:23a). Not only does such a person ignore what the law requires in caring for the poor, he reveals a calloused heart.

Two verses in Proverbs have always been difficult because they apparently contradict each other. At one time wisdom says "not to answer a fool according to his folly"

(26:4*a*), but another time she advises to "answer a fool according to his folly" (26:5*a*). On the surface, these seem to be incompatible. But each one has its own distinctive emphasis. On the one hand, we are not to answer the fool along his line of reasoning. For example, when a fool argues with curses in public and the godly person tries to answer him, the end result will be a shouting match. Only the fool wins in such a situation, and the one who seeks to reprimand him becomes like him. On the other hand, occasions arise when we *must* answer the fool, rebuking him in such a way that others within earshot will realize the foolishness of his words. Only God can give us wisdom to know when or when not to answer a fool. Eventually the world will know when the fool is wrong because his speech will reveal that he has no wisdom in his heart.

THE WHISPERER

Four passages take up the topic of the whisperer's brand of talk. He is one who murmurs rebelliously or maliciously. Such people also slander their victims as they talk about them behind their backs. In Jewish tradition, slander is regarded as killing three people: the one engaged in this vicious practice; the one talked about; and the one to whom the malicious information is imparted.

"Gossip [or, slander] separates close friends" (16:28*b*). His words "are like choice morsels" (18:8*a*), eaten with relish and intense interest (see also 26:22 for a similar statement). Such words find their way into the innermost recesses of the body (that is, the heart), but instead of leaving a person satisfied and thankful, they leave only bitterness and hate. The victim of false information or gossip will find that even his closest friends desert him, and it will take a long time before such wounds can heal.

"Without wood a fire goes out; without gossip [or, slander] a quarrel dies down" (26:20). The synonymous parallelism is quite striking. The whisperer adds fuel to the flames of contention, but when he is no longer around tensions cease.

SPEAKING RASHLY

Unfortunately some people can be completely thoughtless and use "reckless words [that] pierce like a sword" (12:18a). Such thoughtless chatter can deeply hurt family friends, co-workers in the office or factory, and even church members. By contrast, "the tongue of the wise brings healing" (12:18b) to wounds inflicted by the harsh talk of the ungodly. We have to be ever on our guard how we use words because they can either hurt or bless people.

LAZINESS

Wisdom takes up as a specific emphasis the human frailty of laziness. Even believers can succumb to this ailment, procrastinating with what we know God wants us to accomplish. Two exhortations against laziness have already been considered in 6:6, 9, but chapters 10-31 contain more wisdom on the subject.

THE SLUGGARD

Wisdom describes the characteristics of the sluggard, as well as how he acts in particular situations. The lazy one is of no profit to those who would employ him. "As vinegar is to the teeth," harmful to both enamel and the gums, "and smoke to the eyes," blinding them, "so is a sluggard" absolutely useless "to those who send him" (10:26). He can only bring disappointment and heartache to any who would dare employ him, knowing already how he can create mountains of problems. If they do not know the new employee's potential difficulties, they will soon find out. The sluggard finds it a chore to work steadily, has a low image of himself, does not know how to manage his time or how to purchase wisely, and, in general, cannot fit into various areas of life because he has not been diligent enough to learn how to cope.

"The [soul of the] sluggard craves and gets nothing" (13:4a). He certainly has normal desires, but he does not put forth the effort to satisfy them because he is so lazy.

By contrast, "the desires [literally, soul] of the diligent are fully satisfied [or, is made fat]" (13:4b), because diligence yields its rewards when principled people achieve their goals. Even believers have a spiritual goal set before them: "I press on to take hold of that for which Christ Jesus took hold of me. . . . I press on toward the goal to win the prize for which God has called me heavenward in Christ Jesus" (Philippians 3:12, 14).

But the lazy one has no defined objectives in life. He walks slowly because he presumes that "the way" before him "is blocked by thorns" (15:19a). Actually, no such obstruction exists. "The sluggard says, 'There is a lion outside!' or, 'I will be murdered in the streets!'" (22:13). He only *imagines* or *pretends* danger, which provides the excuse for doing nothing.

So lazy is the sluggard that he "buries his hand in the dish" and then "will not even bring it back to his mouth" (19:24). Wisdom provides us with a picture of laziness to the extreme. As another passage suggests, "He is too lazy [or, tired] to bring it [that is, the spoon of food] to his mouth" (26:15b). He would rather go hungry than make the least amount of effort to help himself. Here the wisdom writer has created a hyperbole of laziness, yet the fact remains that once a person becomes lazy, he will find it difficult to break his habits and help himself.

The lazy one does not plow his land at the appropriate time ("in season," lit., "autumn") so he can have a crop later in the spring, a possible reference to winter barley or wheat planted during the previous October (20:4a). He does not plow in late autumn, he rationalizes, because it is too cold, but in actuality the lazy fellow is so afflicted with his malady that he is paralyzed. So when "harvest time" comes, "he looks [or, asks, begs]" (20:4b), but those who have an abundance will not help him. His friends reason that the lazy man's misfortune is the result of his own doing, and therefore they do not want to encourage his laziness. This practice, which on the surface may appear hardhearted, was endorsed by Paul in the New Testament: "We gave you this rule: 'If a man will not work, he shall not eat'" (2 Thessalonians 3:10). Proverbs 20:4 also has modern ramifications: we need to take advantage of our most productive years, lest we have nothing when old age comes. God does not excuse a Christian's laziness.

The lazy person has genuine inner desires, but "the sluggard's craving will be the death of him, because his hands refuse to work. All day long he craves for more and more" (21:25-26a), but he does nothing to gain or accomplish what he inwardly knows must be done. The connection between his heart and his hands and feet is broken. In the end, the lazy fellow not only tragically brings ruin on himself but on his loved ones as well. His fields reflect his malady: "thorns . . . come up everywhere, the ground [is] covered with weeds, and the stone wall [is] in ruins" (24:30-31). His neglected field is an eyesore, compared to neighboring farms where his neighbors have been industrious in their efforts.

All the lazy person likes to do is sleep on his bed. "As a door turns on its hinges," creaking as it moves slowly, so the "sluggard turns on his bed," making it creak noisily (26:14). He does not want to face life, and sleep becomes his refuge and retreat. Yet if one tries to correct this lazy fellow, he only excuses himself with his own rationalizations because he thinks of himself as clever "in his own eyes, . . . wiser . . . than seven men who answer discreetly" (26:16). Since the number seven is considered the perfect number, this is the epitome of what wisdom has to offer. But because the sluggard seeks diligently to justify himself, he has become immune to the best that wisdom could teach him. He is so far beyond what anyone could do for him that only God can change his heart and give him new motives and priorities for life.

Each of us, while not lazy to the extreme, may have our rationalizations and excuses. We have to continually ask ourselves why we become slack and lazy and are not doing what God expects from us. The New Testament reminds us likewise that laziness has no place within the body of the Messiah: "Work with your own hands, just as we told you, so that your daily life may win the respect of outsiders and so that you will not be dependent on anybody" (1 Thessalonians 4:11-12).

SLOTH

Another word for laziness is the feminine form of sluggard (translated "laziness" in the NIV and NASB, and "sloth" or "slothfulness" in the KJV*). This condition "brings on deep sleep" (19:15a), which again is a tragic picture of the lazy person. His desire for sleep can be a cover up so as not to face the problems of life. Because he will not work, this "shiftless man" (lit., the soul of deceit) will eventually become desperate when he suffers hunger (19:15b). Such a person only fools himself. Instead of working for his living as he is supposed to, he only seeks for a place to sleep.

THE NEGLIGENT ONE

This particular word, already translated as "deceit" (see above in 19:15b), is also rendered as "slack" or "loose": "Lazy [or, slack] hands make a man poor" (10:4a). the antithetic parallel serves to sharpen the truth of the first line: "Diligent hands bring wealth" (10:4b), meaning that, when a person is not diligent, he will not have wealth. Again, however, we must remember that such statements are good Old Testament truths where, according to the Mosaic Constitution, God promised untold material blessings when people were obedient to Him; the converse was also true. We cannot read such a truth into the New Testament, however, where the Lord only promised to supply all our *needs* (Philippians 4:19; see again the discussion of 3:9-10).

SLACK

This word pictures one who sinks down or drops. The wisdom writer warns that "one who is slack in his work is brother to one who destroys" (18:9). In other words, the person who lets his daily work slide is kin to one who is a rebel, engaging in sabotage.

Wisdom puts a premium on being diligent and making use of the time God provides. Time flies by quickly,

---

* King James Version.

and we have to constantly pray to the Lord: "Teach us to number our days aright, that we may gain a heart of wisdom" (Psalm 90:12). Paul also reminds us that we are to work while it is yet day and to be "alert and self-controlled" (1 Thessalonians 5:5-8).

FOLLY

The book of Proverbs uses three major words to describe the fool, but in English they are all rendered by one word: "fool."

THE SELF-CONFIDENT ONE (*kesil*)

This Hebrew word is used most often, appearing more than forty times in Proverbs. This kind of fool is dull, obstinate, and would rather choose his own way before he thinks of anyone else. Several occurrences of this word have already been considered (1:22, 32; 3:35; 8:5). But the word pictures conveyed by this term are quite instructive.

The book of Proverbs provides some insights into the makeup and character of this fool. "The folly of fools is deception" (14:8b), that is, they only really deceive themselves. The statement is interesting because of the play on words: the word for "fools" is *kesilim*, whereas the word for "folly" is *'iwelet*, a word to be considered shortly. The fool is not only self-confident and foolish, but going a step further, he is also stupid and stubborn. The wordplay pointedly reminds us to avoid this character.

In another play on words the description of the self-confident fool is considered doubly as stupid: "The folly [*'iwelet*] of fools [*kesilim*] yields to folly [*'iwelet*]" (14:24b). The antithetic parallel contrasted with the first line of the verse sharpens the despicable condition: "the wealth of the wise is their crown" (14:24a). But if fools should amass wealth, their words still remain foolishness, resulting in nothing.

Furthermore, "a fool is hot-headed and reckless" (14:16b), overconfident that what he does is right. While "a rebuke" by a wise person "impresses a man of discernment" (17:10a), no one can beat a rebuke into a fool, even with "a hundred lashes" (17:10b). Far "better to meet a bear robbed of her cubs than a fool in his folly" (17:12), again a play on words where the self-confident one is characterized by his stupidity. The fool in his arrogance simply cannot be contained when he loses his self-control.

"A discerning man keeps wisdom in view" (17:24a) because he desires it, but "a fool's eyes wander to the ends of the earth" (17:24b), thinking he will find some elusive wisdom. The only difficulty is that the fool does not even know how to recognize wisdom and lets it slip by him. Neither does he have any "pleasure in understanding [or, discernment]" (18:2a) because he is smug, always taking delight "in airing his own opinions" (18:2b). The tragedy is that this fool thinks he has no need to learn from anyone else. But when he opens his mouth, it "is his undoing and his lips [that is, the words framed by them] are a snare to his soul" (18:7).

Neither is it "fitting for a fool to live in luxury" (19:10a), if he were permitted to have it or revel in it. The only experience worse than living near the fool is the national tragedy of a slave's attaining the power "to rule over princes" (19:10b). The fool thinks he is somebody, trying to be the mover and shaker of his community. But he will only bring about ruin, much as the slave trying to be a king. And as unlikely as "snow in summer" and as injurious as "rain in harvest, honor is not fitting for a fool" (26:1). The fool who in his self-confidence says, "Me, myself, and I are wonderful," is not fit for any position of leadership requiring wisdom, dignity, and godliness.

We are reminded that the fool is entirely unreliable, and to trust him will only lead to disaster. Anyone who sends "a message by the hand of a fool" will learn that his decision is "like cutting one's feet or drinking violence" (26:6). The latter picture likens the fool to the heavy drinker who makes a nuisance of himself and gets into a fight while in a drunken stupor.

Can the fool be taught anything? Wisdom declares that to put "a proverb into the mouth of a fool" is "like a

lame man's legs that hang limp [that is, are paralyzed]"
(26:7). In another description, "like a thornbush in a
drunkard's hand is a proverb in the mouth of a fool"
(26:9). A normal person will attempt to remove the thorn
from his hand, but the drunkard, because the alcohol in
his system has deadened his pain, will be insensitive to
his condition. Likewise, the fool is insensitive to wisdom.
  As noted in the Introduction, giving honor to a fool is
"like tying a stone in a sling" and then trying to hurl the
stone (26:8). No soldier in his right mind would do such a
thing, but neither is it sane to trust in a fool. "Like an
archer who wounds at random," that is, who shoots his
arrows carelessly, wounding the bystander, "so is he who
hires a fool" (26:10), expecting him to do any kind of
work. Taking a fool into one's business is utterly incon-
ceivable.
  Wisdom also asks the pointed question: "Do you see
a man wise in his own eyes?" (26:12a). She answers herself: "There is more hope for a fool than for him" (26:12b).
The conceited person thinks he knows everything. But
perhaps the fool, if he keeps his mouth shut long enough,
just might learn something. Wisdom reflects further: that
"he who trusts in himself [lit., in his heart] is a fool"
(28:26a). The fool becomes the illustration of the worst
that can happen in life.
  Has wisdom painted such a picture of the fool that he
or she is the worst possible person, never learning the basic lessons of life? Occasions do exist when hope is available for him: "Do you see a man who speaks in haste?
There is more hope for a fool than for him" (29:20). Perhaps if the fool would only learn to keep his mouth shut
and listen carefully, he could learn some wisdom.
  The acts of the self-confident fool. The self-confident
person is recognized by his deeds. "A fool finds pleasure in
evil conduct" (10:23a) and actually enjoys his acts of gross
impropriety. In another play on words, "the heart of fools
[kesilim] blurts out folly [or, 'iwelet, stupidity]" (12:23).
The same word order appears again: "a fool exposes his
folly" (13:16b). In one sense he actually proclaims his stupidity while, second, he displays his sorry condition.

What is even worse, "fools detest turning from evil" (13:19*b*), and "a companion of fools suffers harm" (13:20*b*). When a person walks, that is, lives and speaks with wise people, there is a possibility to be wise; but walking with the fool will only lead to destruction.

"The mouth of a fool gushes folly" (15:2*b*), and his "mouth" continues to feed "on folly" (15:14*b*). The word for "folly" is stupidity, which bubbles forth from the mouth of the fool as water from a spring or well. He does not have a "discerning heart [that] seeks knowledge" (15:14*a*) but, rather, feeds on his own pride and grandeur. On the other hand, the believer is encouraged to learn wisdom from God, even if he does not have much of this world's goods: "better a poor man whose walk is blameless then a fool whose lips are perverse" (19:1). As we have already seen, the man or woman who has wisdom is far richer than any wealthy person simply because the wisdom of God is more precious than silver, gold, and every precious metal (4:14-15).

When a fool persists in his ways and does not listen to reason, wisdom states flatly, "Do not speak to" him because "he will scorn the . . . words" (23:9) of the wise. The fool will only waste your time. When faced with wisdom, "a fool gives full vent to his anger [lit., sends forth all his spirit or temper]" (29:11*a*). He pours out his bitterness with a stream of invectives as water flows from a hydrant. In the end, the fool is like the "dog [who] returns to its vomit" (26:11*a*), eating what is most disgusting. He will only repeat "his folly" (26:11*b*) in a life of stupid actions, losing his temper, and being wise in his own eyes.

All of the descriptions of this kind of fool are intended to teach the naive or inexperienced what to avoid at all costs. Even the more seasoned believer needs to be reminded of what to avoid and how to be like the "wise man [who] keeps himself under control" (29:11*b*).

The suffering of the self-confident fool. "Wisdom reposes in the heart of the discerning" (14:33*a*), contrary to what the fool desires in life. He only learns in a painful way what is wrong: "What use is money in [his] hand" because "he has no desire [lit., heart] to get [or, buy] wisdom" (17:16). In reality, because he refuses to listen and take to heart what God desires for him, he has no capacity to absorb wisdom.

In a still more painful picture, even as "penalties are prepared for mockers," so the fool will suffer "beatings" (19:29). The synonymous parallelism of the passage suggests that the fool mocks wisdom and will pay the penalty for his decisions. Furthermore, if the fool persists in his rebellious ways, wisdom observes that as "a whip for the horse, a halter for the donkey," so there will be "a rod for the backs of fools" (26:3). Even as the horse and donkey have to be directed by compulsion, at times the fool can only be handled by physical restraint. God wants us to learn well and be wise in His ways, not straying from Him and thereby suffering the consequences.

THE ARROGANT, STUPID ONE (*'iwelet*)

This type of fool has already been considered in Proverbs 1:7 and 7:22. He is a step worse than the self-confident one described in the previous section. The term *'iwelet* is used fifteen times, twelve of which are in Proverbs 10-27.

Wisdom provides a number of ways to describe the stupid and arrogant person. "The way of a fool seems right to him [lit., in his own eyes]" (12:15a) because *his own* understanding becomes the guide for the way he desires to walk. On the other hand, "a wise man listens to advice" (12:15b). In his impatience, "a fool shows his annoyance at once" (12:16a), flaring up at anyone or anything who tries to stop him.

Wisdom plays with these words again so as to emphasize a sorry state of affairs: "Folly [*'iwelim*] brings punishment [or, discipline] to fools [*'iwelet*]" (16:22b). By using two words that come from the same form, the truth becomes quite pointed: this kind of fool is in a trap that will destroy him. What a high price to pay to be so stubborn as not to listen to what wisdom desires to teach.

If the fool keeps silent, at least his condition goes undetected. When he "holds his tongue" (lit., closes his lips), he is regarded as "discerning" (17:28b). When he sits in the gate and listens to the wisdom expressed by the elders, the fool looks clever while "he has nothing to say" (24:7b). Perhaps he feels it impossible to learn, but at least he knows enough to keep his mouth shut.

Finally, a very revealing picture: "Though you grind a fool in a mortar, grinding him like grain with a pestle, you will not remove his folly from him" (27:22). Grain and chaff can be separated, but the stupidity of the fool continues to cling to him even after being pounded.

Deeds of the arrogant fool. Even worse are the deeds of this stupid person: "Fools mock at making amends for sin" (14:9a). This arrogant fool even goes so far as to spurn (despise) "his father's discipline" (15:5a). On the other hand, "whoever heeds correction shows prudence" (15:5b).

"Every fool is quick to quarrel" (20:3b), and the arrogant one is a loud-mouth who does not know how to bring peace into a context of confusion. To further describe the vicious talk by a stupid person, wisdom provides a sad picture of the fool: a "stone is heavy and sand a burden" when it is wet, "but provocation by a fool is heavier than both" (27:3).

Judgment of the arrogant fool. God has His way of judging arrogance and willful stupidity. "The chattering fool" (or, "stupid person") can expect, in the end, "ruin" (10:8b). Exactly because he creates an intolerable situation when he boasts in himself and refuses to accept wisdom, he will in the end suffer terrible judgment.

The stupid person who "brings trouble on his family" by not having the foresight to provide for them "will inherit only wind" and end up being a "servant to the wise" (11:29). We need God's wisdom to guide our households rightly and to live righteously in this world. Unless there is a drastic change, the arrogant, stupid person will "die for lack of judgment [lit., lack of heart]" (10:21). Instead of being guided by the advice of righteous and wise people, the fool falls prey to those little better than himself, and he will have very little to show for all his efforts.

THE EMPTY-HEADED FOOL

In the third occurrence of a Hebrew word for "fool" (*nabal*), such a person is not only self-confident and stupid, he is also empty-headed. A good example is Nabal (not even his real name; he is called empty-headed) who acted abominably to David (1 Samuel 25:1-38). Especially was this so when he contemptuously decried his benefactor: "Who is this David?" (v. 10). Even his servants knew his character when they reported back to his wife, Abigail, of how detestable Nabal was to David's servants: "He is such a wicked man that no one can talk with him" (v. 17). This word is used three times in Proverbs.

"Arrogant [or, eloquent] speech [lit., lips] is unsuited to a fool" (17:7a). The empty-headed person does not even know how to speak with any kind of genuine wisdom. Neither does the "father" of such a person have any "joy" in him, only "grief" (17:21). How can parents have any pleasure in the child who has sunk so low as to be not only arrogant and stupid but also a boor? One of the worst things that can happen is when this kind of fool, lacking as he is in moral and spiritual wisdom, grows rich and prosperous (30:22). He becomes a tyrant to everyone around him.

The path of life leads upward for the wise
to keep him from going down to the grave.

Proverbs 15:24

There is a way that seems right to a man,
but in the end it leads to death.

Proverbs 14:12

12

A MATTER OF LIFE AND DEATH

Old Testament thinking on the subject of life concerns itself primarily with the various dimensions of everyday life, though it also includes some consideration of
life after death. Moses, the Prophets, and those responsible for the last part of the Old Testament—the Writings-
—focused largely on how to live righteously in this world.
Their outlook for the future was not so much on life in
heaven as it was for the day when the Messiah would pre-
side over the messianic kingdom.

This consideration must ever be kept in mind because in a study of life and death the book of Proverbs will
reflect what Moses, the Prophets, and the writers of the
Psalms had to say on this subject. In our age, believers an-
ticipate their future with God in heavenly bliss. This is
certainly a biblical hope, but it is only part of the experience the Christian views with anticipation. He must also
take into account life in the future messianic kingdom on
earth (Zechariah 14:16-21), followed by a completely ren-
ovated earth in the eternal state of the "new heavens" and
"new earth" (Revelation 21:1).

LIFE

Two word pictures concerning life, "the fountain of life" and the "tree of life," will be considered first. Then we shall take up other dimensions of the true life: the fear of the Lord; the "path of life"; the connection between the tongue, the heart, and life; and the use of the words "breath" and "life" in the English translations of the book of Proverbs.

A FOUNTAIN OF LIFE

In the Middle East, where it does not rain for seven or eight months of the year (from about April to October), nothing is more refreshing than a cold drink of water on a hot, dry day. Jesus spoke of being rewarded for giving "a cup of cold water" to drink (Matthew 10:42). To enjoy such a cup of cold water in ancient days meant letting down the bucket into a deep well and then pulling it up with considerable effort. The cold water quenched a person's thirst, completely satisfying his craving for water. This common, everyday occurrence provides the picture of what it means to satisfy the deeper spiritual needs in a person's soul that cannot be met by what the coin of this world can buy.

Wisdom proclaims that "the mouth of the righteous is a fountain of life" (10:11a). Just as the water from a fountain or well refreshes the weary, thirsty traveler and irrigates plant life, so the words of the wise refresh the heart and soul of those who hear. When a believer speaks wisely the things of God in practical wisdom, his words give comfort to those who are desperately needy in their souls.

"The teaching of the wise is a fountain of life" (13:14a). From this fountain comes a never-ending source of refreshment from the Lord, and its wisdom enables a person to avoid the snares of death. By following God's directions, which provide true refreshment and life, a person can escape the many problems on earth's vale of tears and even an untimely death. In a similar vein, "the fear of the Lord," described as a "fountain of life," can deliver from the "snares of death" (14:27). While the "fear of the Lord" is a recurring theme in the book of Proverbs, relating to many of life's problems, yet this passage declares that because of a wise fear, we will find refreshment in our spirit and soul and have the strength to live above our difficulties and problems in this world.

The "fountain of life" is related to the person who has "understanding" (or, "common sense"; 16:22a). The one who exhibits a godly common sense enjoys inward spiritual refreshment and is able to offer happiness and joy in his testimony to his co-workers, classmates, friends, or family. Spiritual enjoyment is contagious and makes people hungry and thirsty for what the believer possesses. But the second line in the antithetic parallel demonstrates the contrast of joy because of the fountain of life: "Folly brings punishment to fools" (16:22b).

A TREE OF LIFE

The descriptive term "tree of life" refers to the experience of our first parents in the Garden of Eden. God had commanded Adam and Eve not to partake of the tree of the knowledge of good and evil (Genesis 2:16-17). But tempted by Satan, they disobeyed the Lord and, as a result, were removed from the Garden. One primary reason for their separation from an otherwise idyllic life was that they now had fallen natures and so were not "allowed to reach out . . . and take also from the tree of life and eat, and live forever" (Genesis 3:22b). In a sense, the Lord was merciful by banishing them from the Garden because He did not want Adam and Eve, His special and unique creation, eating from the tree of life in their fallen state and then have no opportunity to be changed inwardly. Instead, ever afterward, substitute atonement offered the only way to enjoy the tree of life.

The picture of a tree suggests the possibility of having a new life that God alone can offer. This is a life that can be enjoyed already in this world and is also the means by which we will enjoy God's presence in a future messianic kingdom, when God creates the new heavens and new earth. Partaking of the tree of life is equated with the knowledge of God in Jesus, which assures the believer of a union with God forever.

"The fruit of the righteous is a tree of life" (11:30*a*). The person designated as righteous in an Old Testament context is the believer. When a person comes to faith, he is declared righteous by God. Although the terms and phraseologies used for calling unbelievers to salvation in the church today are different from what was used in Israel under the Mosaic covenant, Israelis could be and were saved and knew very well what it meant to have a new heart and life. The believers' hearts were circumcised (Jeremiah 4:4), and they had the assurance that their sins were forgiven, as David exclaimed: "As far as the east is from the west, so far has he removed our transgressions from us" (Psalm 103:12). But the tree of life refers to more than the possibility of a person's coming to faith. This particular phrase can also describe the godly experiences of the righteous as he lives for the Lord in this world.

One fruit of what it means to be righteous is found in 11:30*b*: "He who wins souls is wise." In an everyday sense, the wise person who has been declared righteous by God seeks to win friends and followers to his way of life. There is a deeper meaning, however, from a spiritual point of view: the righteous person seeks to so touch the lives of others that they too will enter into the experience of salvation through the sacrificial system of Moses. Once that person is declared righteous, he or she can partake of all that is entailed in the tree of life.

In another practical sense, "the tongue that brings healing is a tree of life" (15:4*a*). The wise person's speech is gentle and kind, soothing hurt or ruffled feelings and bringing healing to a hungry heart and soul. In a spiritual sense, the wise person with the right kind of speech can sincerely help a person hurt by the pressures in this world, offering him or her the better option to know the Lord and serve Him with great blessings.

The description, "tree of life," refers also to physical manifestations: "Hope deferred [that is, drawn out and delayed from day to day] makes the heart sick" (13:12*a*). Too many today are looking for deliverance and hoping that the problems in their little world might be solved, only to become discouraged and disillusioned with all they face. For many, life has not dealt kindly with them. On the other hand, "longing fulfilled [that is, hope realized] is a tree of life"(13:12*b*). Our emotions and our physical well-being benefit. All that is involved in the tree of life, the atonement from sin and satisfaction in the deepest recesses of one's heart and soul, make it possible to realize the fulfillment of our longings. When our sanctuary is in the Lord (see again the discussion on 3:5*a*), our expectations have greater meaning than to trust in the things of this world. Even though God had promised untold material blessings to Israel, yet even in the Mosaic Constitution, people who knew the Lord realized to the fullest that the tree of life experience was what mattered most.

OTHER EXPERIENCES OF LIFE

Fear of the Lord. Two verses relate the fear of the Lord and life: because "the fear of the Lord" is the beginning of knowledge and wisdom, the person who has made this statement the guide to life will be led "to life" (19:23*a*)—that is, not only to eternal life, but also to long life and happiness, resting "content, untouched by trouble" (19:23*b*). Again, we must recognize the promise of material blessings within the Mosaic document that does not necessarily apply today. And yet even today we certainly can know the experience of spiritual life, be at peace with the Lord, and at the same time be at peace with our neighbors.

Wisdom also indicates that "humility and the fear of the Lord bring wealth and honor and life" (22:4). Possibly, the meaning of the verse is that the consequences of humility lead one to have a fear of the Lord. When people within the nation humbled themselves before the Lord, sought His face (2 Chronicles 7:14), and stood in awe before Him, God promised, in accordance with the Covenant of Moses, the physical blessings of riches, honor, and long life. These are the blessings God gave to Solomon after he had been discreet enough to ask for wisdom to govern Israel (1 Kings 3:11-14). Implied in the verse, however, is the spiritual dimension of eternal life as well.

Path, or way, of life. Another familiar emphasis is when the wise person, particularly the believer, walks the right path: "He who heeds [or, guards] discipline shows the way of life" (10:17a). The quality exhibited by such a life is that others will be attracted to it. The Holy Spirit will impress the unbeliever that this is the best possible kind of life. By contrast, "whoever ignores correction leads others astray" (10:17b); he himself is already out of God's will by his attitude and consequently misleads other people.

Wisdom also proclaims that the person who walks "in the way of righteousness" will find "life" (12:28a). Again, from an Old Testament view, this promise is for a long and happy life in this world, and "along that path is immortality [lit., no death]" (12:28b). In one sense, the second line of this passage does not really speak of immortality; the wise person does not pursue those practices that bring about an untimely death. The believer is also mortal and one day will die. Therefore, the deeper meaning of the passage is that we can have the best possible life here and now, and afterwards never be separated from the Lord.

Even David declared that when he came to the end of this life, his hope was to "dwell in the house of the Lord forever" (Psalm 23:6b), where he would be filled "with joy in [His] presence, with eternal pleasures at [God's] right hand" (Psalm 16:11b-c). While there is a great emphasis upon how to live righteously in this world, wisdom also suggests that there is more to life than this earthly existence. Consequently, the unbeliever must give consideration to the life after this one so as to not be eternally separated from God.

Wisdom declares that "the path of life leads upward for the wise to keep him from going down to the grave [*sheol*]" (15:24). The word "upward" implies spiritual life after death, and the believer is warned that he should not fall into the world where people are eternally separated from God. We are encouraged thereby to follow God's wisdom that leads us to a personal experience with Him and to walk the path He has outlined. We can then enjoy the best, not only in this world but also in the next.

A concept parallel to walking the path of righteousness is demonstrated by the one who pursues or is steadfast in righteousness. Wisdom promises that "the truly righteous man attains life" (11:19a). We are, therefore, encouraged as believers to practice righteousness in a continuous, uninterrupted, and unwavering sense. To do so leads to a life that is happy and well-rounded.

The pursuit of "righteousness and love" leads to "life, prosperity [lit., righteousness] and honor" (21:21). What is interesting in this poetic couplet is that the one who *pursues* righteousness (line one) also *finds* "prosperity," literally, righteousness (line two). Obviously, the play on words is for added emphasis. Some Bible scholars have translated the "righteousness" of the second line as "prosperity" (see NIV). Such a translation may well be the better choice. Once again, from an Old Testament context, there is an emphasis upon a full, well-rounded life, enjoying material and spiritual blessings and receiving honor from one's own neighbors and even the nation's leaders. To live righteously, particularly as a genuine Christian, will in most cases be a life of joy and honor even in our day.

The person who pursues righteousness steadfastly is also the one "who listens [intently] to a life-giving reproof" (15:31a). He will be known as wise and "will be at home among . . . wise" people (15:31b). The person who lives godly and wisely will have a testimony in his community and, for the most part, will be greatly respected.

The combination of both Old and New Testament emphases provides for balance between the emphasis on salvation and righteous living. Whereas the Mosaic Covenant greatly emphasized the outcome of salvation, whereby the believer was to demonstrate his love for God and his fellow man by the way he or she lived righteously, preaching in the church today underscores the call for salvation to the unbeliever. This is not to say that encouragement to find atonement in the Mosaic Covenant was absent or that the New Testament has little to say concerning righteous living. Somehow we have to find a balance, affirming that after a person has come to faith he needs to apply the wisdom of the Word of God to live godly in this present generation. The book of Proverbs is a great help to guide the Christian in his life-style so that he or she can reflect the righteousness, love, and compassion of God to the unsaved. When we serve God in the power of His Holy Spirit, we will impact the desperate needs of children growing up in ungodly homes, the teenager who feels there is nothing more to live for in this world, and adults who, hopefully, will realize that their hopes are not fulfilled in money, stock markets, material things, or even robust health.

The tongue, the heart, and life. Wisdom has a lot to say about the way we use our tongues (see chapter 11). James picks up on this theme and develops it even further to encourage or warn what is a proper and improper use of the tongue (James 3). The wisdom writer declares that "the tongue has the power of life and death" (18:21*a*). "Those who love it [that is, make use of the tongue in speech] will eat its fruit" (18:21*b*). The way a person uses the tongue to speak his words can be either for good or for evil. The wise person uses his tongue rightly, earning a reward, but the evil person or fool misuses his tongue to his own hurt and eventual shame. What a powerful lesson for believers today.

A definite relationship exists between the inner person (his heart, psyche, soul) and the function of the physical body. The writer says, "A heart at peace gives life to the body" (14:30*a*). A quiet heart that is not easily agitated can indeed bring healing to the entire body. On the other hand, "envy rots the bones" (14:30*b*), and because the word "bones" stands parallel to "body" in line one, the parallel in line two refers not only to rotten bones but to a breakdown in the entire bodily mechanism—the organs, the glandular output, the flesh, and so on.

Two other occurrences of the word "life" describe the "favor" of the king that is extended toward the servant who deals wisely (16:15). To have such favor means life indeed for the recipient, whereas to arouse the king's wrath by rebellion or any other unwise deeds can bring death (16:14a). The righteous person enjoys the king's favor, which is "like a rain cloud in spring" (16:15b). The simile refers to the latter rains in the springtime, which help to ripen the grain. Therefore, as the godly person serves the civil authority righteously, he not only has his blessing, but the believer is a testimony to unbelievers. In another place "life" is that which describes the activity of the godly woman: "All the days of her life" she does her husband "good, not harm" (31:12).

Breath, soul, and life. Another parallel use of the word "life" employs the Hebrew word *nefesh*, variously translated, "breath," "soul," or "life." Obviously, a connection exists between all three terms. *Nefesh* refers to the center of one's very being, wherein lie the memory and the motivations for choices in life (see discussion of 1:18-19, 6:26, 7:23).

Wisdom approves of the person who "guards his lips," suggesting that by such a decision, he also "guards his soul" (13:3a). As in chapter 11, the one who is extremely careful about what he speaks guards his life. However, "the one who speaks rashly [lit., opens wide his lips] will come to ruin" (13:3b).

In another verse this Hebrew word pictures how "a man's riches may ransom his life" (13:8a). When a rich man is confronted by robbers and thieves who want his money, or when deceitful officials are looking for bribes, it may be best for him to give up part or all of his money. After all, which is more important, the life that is infinitely precious or money and position that even in ordinary circumstances can vanish by daybreak? Such advice is good for today should one face the prospect of being mugged on the streets. Money can be replaced, but how can a life be restored?

There is also a lesson concerning how "a righteous man [that is, the believer] cares for the needs of his animal" (12:10a). The reason he treats his beast of burden kindly is because he is concerned for its life. One of the Jewish lessons concerning the care of animals taught that a person was not to eat his own food before he had fed his animals.

DEATH

Of the fourteen passages that deal with death, five have already been considered in places where the use of antithetic parallelism dealt with life. These are first repeated here briefly to highlight the contrast with life.

DEATH CONTRASTED WITH LIFE

The opposite of "the truly righteous man" who "attains life" (11:19a) is the unbeliever "who pursues evil and goes to his death" (11:19b). This verse pictures the person who continually makes wrong choices, pursues after evil, and dies miserably. It implies eternal separation from God. To pursue righteousness is life, "and along that path is immortality [lit., no death]" (12:28). There are also two warnings to turn aside from the "snares of death" (13:14b; 14:27), and the person who misuses his tongue experiences death (18:21).

THE WAY OF DEATH

A well-known general statement concerns the person who walks in "a way that seems right . . . but . . . leads to death" (14:12; 16:25). Imagine the person who sets out on a path that appears to be leading to the right destination but discovers that it leads him to danger. Only the wise find the right way, and the wisdom that enables him or her to be on the right road comes only from God. Jesus also distinguished between the broad way and the narrow way. The broad way leads to destruction; the narrow way "leads to life," into the presence of God (Matthew 7:13-14). We are warned to walk in the way outlined by God, which in many cases is not necessarily the most popular road to take.

THE USE OF MONEY

The handling of money has always been a snare to people. The wisdom writer warns that "ill-gotten treasures are of no value [lit., do not profit] but righteousness delivers from death" (10:2). The phrase "do not profit" stands in perfect parallel with "death." Money acquired through wickedness (see 10:14, for example) may give temporary pleasure, but such "treasures of wickedness" will be worthless when one is called upon to give an account of his deeds before God. The only dynamic that can deliver from the love of money that leads to death is wisdom, who stands ready to guide the believer in righteous deeds approved by God. After all, wisdom is more precious than all the money in the world. Why, then, should people make wrong choices regarding what is real wealth?

Similarly, "wealth is worthless in the day of wrath, but righteousness delivers from death" (11:4). Whatever wealth one may have accumulated during his lifetime will not avail on the day of judgment when God reviews the deeds of people. Bribes may blunt right judgment by human judges, but no one will be able to sway God's justice. Again, wisdom underscores strongly the decision to do what is righteous. But it is even more important that one be declared righteous in *salvation* so that human interests alone, and money in particular, will not be the sole aim in life.

Wisdom warns further concerning attaining riches by "a lying tongue" (21:6). Such schemes to acquire wealth are useless and lead only to death. Furthermore, these ill-gotten gains will be like a fleeting vapor, reminding us that stolen treasure can disappear quickly into thin air.

In no way should it be understood that the book of Proverbs condemns wealth. Rather, the warning is against obtaining it through trickery. Paul also warned concerning the misuse of money, the love of which leads into "all kinds of evil. "Because of an inordinate love for money, many have "pierced themselves with many griefs" (1 Timothy 6:10). When people make money their god, it will not avail in the end to help them face an eternity separated from those values that are eternal and matter the most.

THE END OF THE WICKED

Wisdom provides three individual warnings concerning what will happen to the wicked. In one sense, the wicked "are brought down . . . when calamity comes . . . but even in death the righteous have a refuge" (14:32). Whoever follows a life of wickedness will be overtaken when calamity strikes him, for he has nothing to fall back on for support. He or she will be overwhelmed by life's circumstances and in the end will perish. However, the righteous person has found salvation and lives according to a wisdom provided by God. The believer will be steadied by his or her faith even when the pressures of life seem insurmountable. And even when death comes for the believer, he or she will find hope and have complete assurance for the hereafter.

THE NEIGHBOR

Wisdom carefully describes the kind of person who would deceive his neighbor, either by lying to him, slandering him behind his back, or trying to cheat him in a business deal, as "a madman shooting firebrands or deadly arrows" (26:18-19a). When confronted by his neighbor about such stupid behavior, the offender replies, "I was only joking" (26:19b).

COMMUNITY SENSITIVITY

Those within the community of Israel were always to regard themselves as their brother's keeper. Wisdom enjoins people to make the attempt to "rescue those being led away to death" (24:11a). The passage can refer to either innocent prisoners about to be unjustly executed or to those facing imminent danger. The person in close contact with the authorities should attempt to intercede on behalf of an innocent victim. He should not remain silent and do nothing in such circumstances.

Finally, when a king or a ruling authority is displeased with the unwise, "the king's wrath is a messenger of death" (16:14a) and only "a wise person will appease" the king's displeasure (16:14b). Most of the time, the wise person tries to find favor before a "king's face," which is as "life" itself (16:15a). Peter and Paul remind us that we need to be obedient as much as possible "to the governing authorities" and to pray for them so there can be peace in the community (Romans 13:1-5; 1 Timothy 2:1-2; 1 Peter 2:13-15).

Obviously there are occasions when a governmental authority meddles with our conscience, asking that we give up our faith. We then have to say that no government can penetrate into these areas. For example, Peter had to take his stand before the highest tribunal in his country when his beliefs were questioned: "We must obey God rather than men!" (Acts 5:29). Evil governments have decreed race genocide, as Pharaoh did in ancient Egypt when he ordered the death of all male infants (Exodus 1:16), or as the National Socialists in Germany under Hitler when they proposed their solution to the Jewish question by ordering all Jewish people to be killed. Such governments have become immoral because they violate the sanctity of life and flout God's standards of justice. Believers cannot stand idly by and refuse to help people who have been so grossly victimized. But one fact needs to be considered: when we do take a stand for righteousness in such circumstances, it can cost us our lives.

CONCLUSION

The book of Proverbs is an extremely practical study, particularly for believers, providing advice on how to live in this present life. The Old Testament writers, as they spoke on behalf of wisdom, wanted everyone to enjoy life at its best. Occasions do exist, however, when we suffer in conditions and circumstances beyond our control. Yet through prayer and seeking God's wisdom, we can still enjoy a vibrant life that will contribute greatly to peace in the community and will be a testimony to unbelievers.

Such a life-style will interest many in the claims of the truth of His Word. May God grant us His wisdom in the power of Jesus Christ for our well-being and the salvation of both family and friends and for His own glory.

BIBLIOGRAPHY

Alden, Robert L. *Proverbs: A Commentary on an Ancient Book of Timeless Advice.* Grand Rapids: Baker, 1983.

Delitzsch, Franz. *Proverbs–Song of Solomon.* Vol. 6 of *Commentary on the Old Testament,* by C. F. Keil and F. Delitzsch. Grand Rapids: Eerdmans, 1973.

Gaebelein, A. C. *The Holy Scriptures Analyzed, Proverbs.* New York: Our Hope, 1921.

Greenstone, J. H. *Proverbs with Commentary.* Philadelphia: Jewish Publication Society of America, 1950.

Ironside, H. A. *Notes on the Book of Proverbs.* Neptune, N.J.: Loizeaux, 1907.

Jones, Edgar. *Proverbs and Ecclesiastes.* London: S.C.M., 1961.

Kidner, Derek. *The Proverbs: An Introduction and Commentary.* Downers Grove, Ill.: InterVarsity, 1964.

MacDonald, William. *Listen, My Son.* Kansas City: Walterick, 1965.

McKane, W. *Proverbs, a New Approach.* Old Testament Library. London: S. C. M., 1970.

Morgan, G. Campbell. *Practical Wisdom.* Analyzed Bible. New York: Revell, 1908.

Perowne, T. T. *The Book of Proverbs.* Cambridge: University, 1899.

Santa, George F. *A Modern Study in the Book of Proverbs*. Milford, Mich.: Mott Media, 1978.

Scott, R. B. Y. *Proverbs/Ecclesiastes*. Anchor Bible. New York: MacMillan, 1971.

_____. *The Way of Wisdom in the Old Testament*. New York: MacMillan, 1971.

Toy, C. H. *A Critical and Exegetical Commentary on the Book of Proverbs*. Edinburgh: T. & T. Clark, 1899.

Wardlaw, Ralph. *Lectures on the Book of Proverbs*. London: Fullerton, 1861. Reprint. Minneapolis: Klock and Klock, 1981.

Whybray, R. *The Book of Proverbs*. Cambridge: University, 1972.